Shifting Scenes

Irish Theatre-Going, 1955-1985

John Devitt

in conversation with

Nicholas Grene and Chris Morash

A Carysfort Press Book

Shifting Scenes
Irish Theatre-Going, 1955-1985

First published as a paperback in Ireland in 2008
by Carysfort Press Ltd
58 Woodfield, Scholarstown Road, Dublin 16, Ireland
ISBN 978-1-904505-33-3

Printed and bound by eprint limited
Unit 35, Coolmine Industrial Estate, Dublin 15, Ireland

Cover design by Alan Carmody

Typeset by Alan Carmody

Front and back cover photographs courtesy of Ros Kavanagh©

This book is published with the financial assistance of The Arts Council
(An Chomhairle Ealaíon), Dublin, Ireland

John Devitt was born in Dublin in 1941. He was educated by the Christian Brothers at O'Connell's School and was a graduate (English and Classics) of UCD. His teaching career began in 1963 in Glenstal Abbey. He later taught at St. Joseph's CBS in Fairview before becoming head of English at the Mater Dei Institute of Education in 1979, a post he held until his retirement in 2006. He regularly reviewed books, films and plays for a range of Irish journals and newspapers, radio and television programmes. The theatre was a lifelong passion, one he shared generously. John Devitt died in June 2007.

Nicholas Greene is Professor of English Literature at Trinity College, Dublin.

Chris Morash is Professor of English at NUI Maynooth.

Contents

Illustrations

Illustrations (continued)

Illustrations (continued)

Acknowledgements

We gratefully acknowledge the financial support that made this project possible: in Trinity College, Dublin from the School of English and the Provost's Academic Development Fund; in the National University of Ireland, Maynooth, the Publication Fund, and the School of English, Media and Theatre Studies. Permissions for reproduction of images used in the book are included in the list of Illustrations.

The book is John Devitt's and its purpose is to record his unique memories of theatre-going in Ireland, but it was from first to last a collaborative enterprise and we are most grateful to all those who helped to bring it together. Sinéad O'Donnell, as our highly efficient sound engineer, made an agreeable fourth at our original interviews with John. With admirable patience and conscientiousness, Denis Condon took on the time-consuming and demanding task of transcribing the ten hours of tapes that resulted from the interviews. We are grateful to Jim Keenan, cartographer and cultural historian, who produced the map of John Devitt's Dublin, and to the staff of the Russell Library at NUI Maynooth, who accorded John's film-goer's diary the same treatment as a medieval manuscript. We owe a special debt of gratitude to Alan Carmody who not only acted as our picture researcher but as the designer of the book, re-setting it again and again through multiple edited versions. Lisa Coen also carried out detailed research for us with characteristic energy and resourcefulness. Dan Farrelly, Eamonn Jordan and Lilian Chambers at Carysfort Press have been very positive in their support for the project.

We would not have gone forward with this book without the encouragement of Irene Devitt; we hope that for her, and for all the other members of John's family, it represents one means of remembering him. For theatre scholars who wish to consult the original interviews, we have deposited full copies of the tapes in the Oscar Wilde Centre for Irish Writing, School of English, Trinity College, and in the Library, NUI Maynooth.

For help in sourcing illustrations we wish to thank Justin Furlong of the National Library of Ireland, Mary Clarke of the Dublin City Libraries, Mairead Delaney, Jimmy Fay and Jessica Traynor of the Abbey Theatre.

Nicholas Grene
Chris Morash

Preface

I first met John Devitt when in the early 1980s he enrolled as a student on what was then a graduate diploma course in Anglo-Irish literature in Trinity College, Dublin. After my lectures a tall, ruggedly-built man with a slight scholar's stoop, an eager, engagingly vital manner and an innate intellectual courtesy, would ask the kind of penetrating, sometimes unsettling questions that quickly made me realize that he could himself have been giving the lectures with which he engaged so generously during that early stage of our friendship. He had taken a year out from his own professional career as teacher and lecturer and brought to the classroom exchanges and after-lecture discussions in Trinity a sensibility that was already unselfconsciously confident about matters of taste and about the fundamental values such confidence involved. These certitudes I quickly came to understand were based on an impressive knowedge of the classics and of modern literature but also on John's dedicated attendance over many years at as many plays and films as his busy life as teacher, academic Head of a Department and family man allowed. They were also based on an unusual combination of attributes: a formidable, restless, critical intelligence, a capacious recollection of and appreciation for aesthetic achievement, and boundless enthusiasm for many areas of human activity. So, over the years, I was to learn that John not only loved the theatre and cinema with an irrepressible passion but also hurling and cricket (he had in fact been something of a force as a fast bowler in his youth). His approach to things of the mind, to the literary and dramatic arts, was that of the fully-formed human being whose sense of life as a troubling yet exhilarating adventure seemed to increase as the years ran on, when the enthusisam and mental curiosity I recognised in him at our first meeting showed no sign of waning. He was both a resource and an inspiration, a presence in Dublin's cultural life whose judgement was respected and whose companionable, always vigorously conducted conversation was sought out by all who knew how special he was.

It is a measure of the respect that John Devitt enjoyed as just such a resource and inspiration that two of Ireland's foremost theatre historians and critics, Nicholas Grene and Chris Morash, should have made it their business to create the archive of recorded conversations with John about theatre in Dublin between 1955-1985, upon which this book is based. Its publication must have its poignant aspect, since, based as it is on live recordings, it reminds us that John passed away in June of 2007, and that the voice we can hear so persuasively in the pages of this volume has sadly been silenced. Indeed, one senses that the knowledge that John had suffered serious ill-health and that the prognosis might be uncertain gave an undeniable urgency to the work of record thoughtfully undertaken by Grene and Morash. All those interested in the Dublin and Irish theatre must therefore be grateful to them that they have made possible this publication in which a vivid personality and rich, accumulated experience are extended beyond the circle who knew John Devitt in his lifetime. For those who did know him it serves also as a fitting memorial and testament to the regard in which he was deservedly held as dedicated teacher, gifted conversationalist and loyal friend.

The world in which John Devitt as a young man became, in his own words, 'seriously besotted with the theatre' was a very different one to that which exists today. Dublin was a small, intimate city with its memories of stirring revolutionary times, settling into a sense of its distinctive post-independence identity. John's mother (as John narrates it here) before her marriage was present for the famously stormy reception of *The Plough and the Stars* in 1926, and despite what other reports record of that tumultuous night, managed to hear what Yeats had to say, before she wisely departed, fearing a really dangerous riot. By the 1950s the predominantly lower-middle-class audiences at the Abbey (and Devitt is clear on how theatre-going was essentially 'a lower-middle-class passion' in the Dublin of his boyhood and young manhood) had become accustomed by contrast to a staple of plays such as those by the immensely popular John McCann, the function of whose plays was to offer reassurance to playgoers. They could be assured that, despite the emigration that was emptying streets in such Dublin lower-middle-class suburbs as Drumcondra (where Devitt's parents made their home) as families took the boat for pagan England and economic survival, all was essentially well in a society defined by devout Catholicism, respect for national institutions such as the GAA and Aer Lingus (then a focus of patriotic pride) and communal support for the state. Yet many in the audiences for McCann's plays and others like them, in which the myth of pagan England was propagated, would, as Devitt insists, have had relatives in England and would therefore have known that the myth was nonsense. Furthermore, 'many people' like himself who 'would have had a sacramental view of Christianity and of the world' were also dogged by 'a nagging suspicion that maybe there was no God after all'. Consequently Dublin audiences could not always be satisfied by anodyne drama that only 'administered reassurance'. Over the years, therefore, there was a steady constituency for such remarkable theatrical events as Frank Dermody's production of O'Neill's *Long Day's Journey Into Night* or Tomás Mac Anna's production of Brecht's *Galileo* (both hailed as high points in this book) when drama directly confronted controversial matters (in the former the sanctity of the family, in the latter the conflict between authority and freedom of enquiry). And one of the particular pleasures of *Shifting Scenes* is the sense John Devitt communicates of the Dublin of the 1950s, so often characterised as a period of unmitigated tedium, as an 'eager talkative city' in which drama on stage and on the air-waves (both Radio Éireann and the BBC radio drama commanding wide listenerships) was a topic of conversation in pubs after the curtain fell, in bus queues and in places of work next day. Devitt believed that 'the creation of an audience is one of the great things theatre does'. By the evidence he presents it is made clear that theatre in Dublin created and held an audience for exciting, significant drama in the 1950s and 1960s, an audience which perhaps metamorphosed in the 1970s and 1980s, but which can scarcely be said to exist in this century.

Shifting Scenes is full of Devitt's enthusiasm and gratitude for the theatrical personalities, dramatists, actors and directors, who made his constant quest over the decades for authentic dramatic experience a kind of lifetime avocation. Here we learn of Cyril Cusack's Hamlet, of Mac Líammóir's Iago, of Godfrey Quigley's Macbeth as compared with Anew McMaster in the Scottish Play, of Ria Mooney in *Long Day's Journey Into Night*. We are taken back to charged evenings when modern classics such as *Philadelphia, Here I Come!, The Gigli Concert, Talbot's Box, Faith Healer, Observe the Sons of Ulster Marching Toward the Somme* were new-minted, theatrical experiments, daringly extending the range of Irish theatre. And it is full of Devitt's bold conversational style in which a zest for comic anecdote is mingled with exasperated impatience for the shoddy and second rate (he lavished praise where he felt it due but could be colourfully damning of mediocrity). Here too are the brilliant aperçus, almost offhandedly tossed off, which made his talk a heady affair, as when he observes of O'Casey's *The Plough and the Stars* (which, unlike some current academic critics, he regarded as a masterpiece) that it 'shifts gear and uses different technical means in each act, and generalises itself superbly at the end.' But even with such a work of genius his critical faculty remained fully engaged.

He recognised that the love scenes are weak in that play, and comments with exacting acumen of a youthful amateur production: 'maybe you can get away with the love scenes if moon-faced stricken creatures play it.'

Devitt's engagement with theatre as an art form was rooted, as this volume makes evident, in what must be termed a religious view of the world. He was haunted by moments in life when a community of people – actors at work with a skilled director, a repertory company whose ensemble voice-music could make high art of an everyday radio play, even the spectacle of crowds at Croke Park present at 'dynamic, dramatic occasions' – were touched by something beyond themselves. These moments seemed to offer him glimpses of some kind of transcendence. The best of them were experienced in the theatre, when it proffered 'that lovely duet, faith and doubt' in a context of 'a shared sense of what is important'. A telling definition of theatre which he provides here indicates that what Devitt valued most as an inveterate playgoer were occasions when the sum was greater than the parts: 'That's theatre', he affirms like a credo, 'when the available means are far out of proportion to the effect produced. There is no way of explaining it, it's a real mystery'.

There is a fascinating thesis advanced in the pages of this book about the role of drama in Irish society in the later twentieth century, a thesis that I believe will be taken up by future cultural historians of the period (and this alone makes it a valuable document). It is a thesis that emerges from Devitt's appreciation of how that society was underpinned by a religious consensus (in which he shared) that from the mid-1960s and early 1970s underwent a process of dissolution. It was that consensus, formed by influences such as catechetics in the schools, that meant that Irish audiences in the 1950s possessed an awareness of drama's religious dimension and had accordingly no difficulty, for example, in grasping how deeply Shakespeare was affected by a Catholic sacramentalism even as the

England of his day became officially Protestant. It allowed, indeed, John Devitt's own family to accept as 'self-evident', in a way closed off to more secular folk, that Brendan Behan's *The Quare Fellow*, in its communal horror of capital punishment as an atrocious act directed against the body, derives some of its power from the fact that its subtext 'was the religious mystery of the body of Christ.' Devitt reckons this religious ethos, which could invest Behan's play with religious significance for Irish audiences, as it dissolved, gave a special quality to Irish theatre from about 1973 to 1985, when a huge religious and cultural change took place. He asks, in a brilliantly stimulating question (the kind I remember him posing in Trinity when I first met him): 'Is the theatre the art form of the eleventh hour, when some things are fading, and other things are replacing them, but the things that are fading are still vestigial presences?' And Chris Morash immediately grasps the explanatory force of this possibility when he comments in excited reply: 'It would make sense with a play like *Sanctuary Lamp*, it would make sense of *Talbot's Box*, it would make sense even with *Faith Healer*, which we keep coming back to.' It is as if Morash anticipates the book that John Devitt's insight might inspire and in so doing reminds us of how crucial it is that we should have this permanent record of a remarkable man's memories and observations made available to us.

Terence Brown
November, 2007

Introduction

Theatre is the ephemeral art.

As anyone who has ever struck a set, or taken a final curtain call on a closing night, will know, when a production of a play finishes its run, it is gone. All that remains when the stage is swept for the last time is a thin trail of newspaper clippings, promptbooks, scripts – and memories. Of these traces left by the performance, the memories of audience members are arguably the most important; most of the other traces are left by theatre professionals, whether they be writers, directors, designers or critics, and as such they are mulled over by later historians and commentators. However, in any place where a play is being performed, most of the people in the room are not theatre professionals; they are the audience, people who have paid their money to see a play. It may be a cliché to say that without the audience, there is no play. Yet, at the same time, it is the audience who are usually the most fully lost to history.

For theatre historians, the recognition that we are writing about something that is, by definition, gone and ultimately unrecoverable is the elephant in the room. Unlike the literary critic, or the art historian, who can write with the object of their analysis before them, the theatre historian is always writing about something that is, by definition, missing. And, of course, the same is true of any person who finds oneself in a room with other theatre-goers, trying to conjure up performances from the past, much as Gabriel Conroy in Joyce's 'The Dead' tries to conjure up the voices of long-gone singers.

Considerations such as these may sound like arcane, highly theoretical matters, and the fact of the matter is that most people who write about theatre simply acknowledge the problem, and get on with the business of writing and talking about plays. And, for the most part, we do so by necessity, for while scripts can be taken down from library shelves, and theatre reviews can be ferreted out of archives, memories other than our own are not as easily retrieved, except in the cases of rare individuals. John Devitt was that rare individual.

Over the years, both of us – and, indeed, many others writing about Irish theatre as well – had a secret weapon in the theatre historian's struggle against the forgetfulness that constantly threatens to swallow up any given performance from the past. When writing about, for instance, the 1959 Abbey production of Eugene O'Neill's *Long Day's Journey into Night*, or Tomás Mac Anna's 1966 production of Brecht's *Galileo*, or Tom Murphy's *The Gigli Concert*, the first step was to do the dutiful research: look at the press clippings, find whatever posters or programmes or other bits and pieces might have survived. Then, over the years, both of us would have reached for the telephone, to ask John what those productions were really like.

John Devitt started attending the Dublin theatre sometime in the late 1940s, and among his earliest memories are productions in the original Abbey Theatre, which was destroyed by fire in 1951. As he recounts in the interviews presented here, he grew up on the North side of Dublin, at a time vibrant with talk. Even though his father's job as a Guard may not have left much in the way of disposable income, John managed, nonetheless, to go to the theatre, and to the cinema, with a frequency that would put to shame many of us living in more prosperous times. As he remembers those years here, going to the theatre (and to the cinema, and listening to plays on the radio) was as important as eating or drinking; it was the cultural air that he breathed, and one could no more have considered joining in the conversation at the bus stop without having heard the Sunday radio play, or having watched the Abbey's latest offering, than one would consider appearing at the bus stop naked.

In these interviews about his earliest theatre-going, John challenges – quite openly – the common preconception that what has become known as 'De Valera's Ireland' was a grey dreary cultural wasteland. In the past year, books by Clair Wills and Diarmuid Ferriter have asked us to rethink the ways in which we imagine those years. For John, that process was one that went on for his whole life. While he was far too unsentimental to harbour any notions of 'rare oul times', and vividly recalls demonstrators being met with baton charges, and mountains of turf piled up in the Phoenix Park to give to the poor, at the same time he maintains that the Dublin in which he grew up was far from culturally dead. It was a 'talking town', he insists. The Dublin of the 1950s may not have left many great monuments behind, but that was because it defined itself through cultural forms that were ephemeral: talk – and theatre. John's tough-minded refusal to accept the received wisdom on those years was, in many ways, typical of his lively and combative mind, shaped and honed by years of teaching, reading, reflecting and talking.

John could not only articulate – forcefully, eloquently, and with great wit – the view that Dublin in the 1950s had a distinctive, and vigorous, cultural life; he could back up his argument with impressive powers of recall. Theatrical performances that made an impression on him stayed with him. He could talk about Ria Mooney's performance in the 1959 production of *Long Day's Journey into Night*, or Godfrey Quigley in the 1983 production of *The Gigli Concert* not as events from forty-five or twenty-five years ago, but as if he had just walked out of the theatre, with the long-gone actors' faces vividly before him.

In this respect, John Devitt is like Joseph Holloway, the tireless theatre-goer and diarist who lived in Dublin in the first half of the twentieth century. From the early 1890s until his death in 1944, Holloway went to the theatre almost every evening, often seeing the same production two or three times, and recording his impressions of the theatre in a diary. Now held in the Manuscripts Collection of the National Library of Ireland, the Holloway diaries run to something like 25 million words. It would be impossible to imagine writing about the Irish theatre of those years without them, for they provide an otherwise lost sense of what it was actually like to sit in a theatre and watch a play in 1904 or 1926. In a sense, John Devitt picks up where Holloway left off, inheriting his massive, indefatigable enthusiasm for the theatre, his willingness to travel across the city to small, ill-equipped rooms, simply to watch theatre, and his willingness to watch the same production over and over again, as if trying to fully understand the magic of a great performance.

In two respects, however, John Devitt was completely unlike Joseph Holloway. In the first place, all of the hours that Holloway spent in the theatre did little to blunt his ability to misjudge a play. Synge's *Playboy of the Western World*, which he saw in its tumultuous first week, he thought smutty, and he frequently suggested to Yeats that melodrama was the theatrical model to emulate. In this respect, John was completely unlike Holloway, in that he had an informed and finely tuned critical sense, and his conviction of the value of certain key plays is surefooted, and sharpened by the years.

The other respect in which John differed from Joseph Holloway was that while Holloway left a written record of his theatre-going that is breath-taking in its sheer scale, John's memories remained a part of the oral culture of a talking town in which he grew up. The present book arose from a recognition, building with each passing year, that John Devitt's memories of the theatre were a part of Ireland's theatrical heritage, and should be preserved in some format, in much the same spirit as Holloway's diaries are carefully kept under the guardianship of the National Library. In the summer of 2005, we began discussing with John the possibility of recording a series of interviews, and soon the project grew into a book. The process of recording, with the help of sound engineer Sinéad O'Donnell, took place over a series of winter evenings in 2006, and was a kind of performance in its own right. John was a skilled raconteur, and often it required only the gentlest nudges from either of us to keep the words flowing. As much as it was possible to do so, we have tried to preserve the quality of John's voice in the editing of those interviews. The initial process of transcription, undertaken by Denis Condon, produced a manuscript of more than 100,000 words, which we have reduced down to the present form. While we were working on the final edited version of the interviews, John died in June of 2007. In publishing these interviews, we are making a small protest against the necessary, and in some senses tragic, ephemerality of two things that meant so much to John Devitt: the theatre, and talk.

Nicholas Grene
Chris Morash

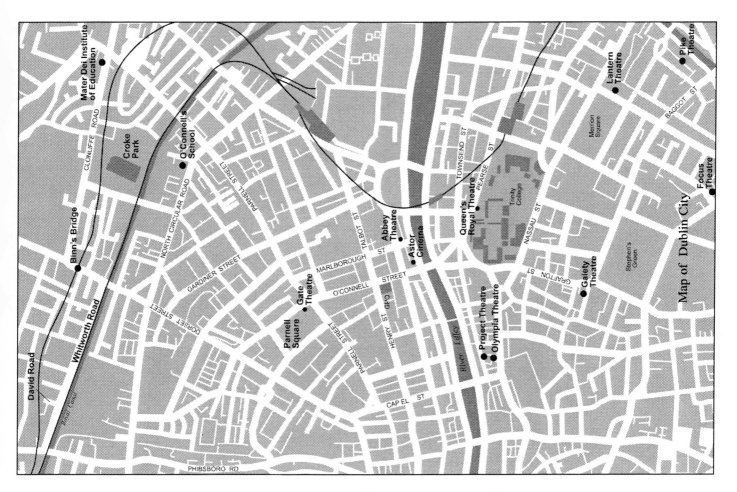

Map of Dublin City

Chapter 1

Growing up in 1950s Dublin

Brendan Behan Memorial on the
Royal Canal near Binns Bridge

NG: We might start by asking you about your earliest memories, your background, how you came to go to the theatre so much.

JD: My earliest memory is of a bomb shelter on Binns Bridge and watching it being demolished and enjoying it being demolished. People take as much pleasure in kicking a sandcastle to pieces as they do in making it. And I've always responded to Yeats in that way. Yeats's understanding of imagination is not that of a tame child who can be relied on to be creative: it's a very destructive and creative business simultaneously. Bid me strike a match and blow!

Another early memory is of a baton charge, also on Binns Bridge. I grew up in a cul-de-sac on the Whitworth Road and went to O'Connell's School, about a mile away. And coming home from school one day I saw the tail end of a baton charge. People were demonstrating on the banks of the Royal Canal in protest against the jailing of an unemployed man who'd been elected T.D. The baton charge was launched from Cross Guns Bridge, and by the time the police got to Binns Bridge, they were berserk. My father was a Guard and I went home and told him what happened. He nearly went bananas; he said that there was no need for that. When you launch a baton charge you may well have a purpose in mind. But the people who start lashing out very quickly part with any purpose. A disciplined baton charge is a complete contradiction in terms.

NG: About how old would you have been then, John?

JD: About 14 I'd guess … I would have been about five when the demolition work took place. I pass that spot literally every day of my working life, and it's not possible for me not to remember it.

NG: So do you remember the first time you were in a theatre?

JD: Oh yes. The first time I was in a theatre was in the old Abbey before it burnt down. They were doing a show in Irish and I was at a school where we did everything through Irish so I was fluent in the language. One of our near neighbours was Bill Foley: I lived in 4 David Road, Bill Foley and his family lived in number 2. I heard he was in the Abbey Irish-language panto – they call it now the *geamaireacht*. So I thought, I have to go and see this guy I see at the bus stop. And I went to the theatre, into the middle of the gallery; it was right on the top of the house, but in fact you were very close to the stage. I don't remember the story of the panto but there was an episode set in the Wild West and Bill Foley was clad all in black, with a black hat and a black bootlace hanging down his chin and he was menacing the principal boy and the principal girl. What narrative logic brought them to this pass I no longer recall, but he was very, very impressive. A few years later I saw *Shane* where Jack Palance plays an extraordinarily similar role in just the same canonicals. And I thought, has Jack Palance seen Bill Foley?

NG: Jack's Irish was better than you thought it was.

Jack Palance in *Shane*.
Paramount Pictures.1953

24

JD: There is a point to that story because it made me realize that, anywhere people were pretending to be something else, whether it was in the theatre or in the cinema or even on the radio, I wanted to be around where people were pretending, I wanted to be in on that. And so did everybody else that I knew, including my companions at school, our neighbours and, of course, my mother. My mother was a great theatre-goer as a young girl; she was very frequently in the Abbey. In fact, she was in the Abbey on the Thursday night of the famous riots.

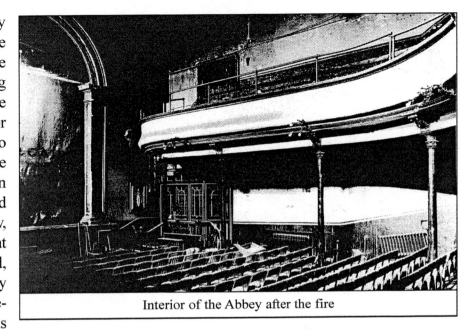

Interior of the Abbey after the fire

CM: *The Plough and the Stars.*

JD: Yes, so I used to get that story once a year, a completely different story from the one that is canonized in theatre histories. She heard Yeats's speech; the widely-repeated idea that Yeats's speech was absolutely inaudible is total bullshit. My mother was there with a friend of hers called Winnie Heaney – this was before my mother married – and after Yeats's speech, she was looking around and she realized that there were men in trench coats with bulges in their coat pockets. And she was convinced that they were going to start firing. Yeats's speech was seriously incendiary; it wasn't designed to placate – oil on troubled waters it was not. And so she said to Winnie, 'Winnie, we better get out of here.' Her version was confirmed by the actor Gabriel Fallon, who also lived right around the corner from us; we shared a bus stop. I used to get the story from Fallon, and it's almost word for word the same account he gives in his book on O'Casey. He was the guy to whom Yeats was talking before the curtain went up. And the story that he told in the book was exactly the same as the story he had told 10 or 12 or 14 years ago at the bus stop.

My mother told another story from I guess around the same time, but I cannot tell you what the play was. She went to the gallery and she was looking down and there was Yeats, as he so often was. She thought he was a terrible snob because he was looking around at the audience as if looking down his nose at them. Then the word came up to the gallery, please come down to the stalls because there weren't enough people in the stalls for the actors to play to. They were delighted: you see, it cost 3/6 to get into the stalls; it cost 1/6 to get to the gallery. So they were getting into the 3/6 penny seats. Yeats starts up again repeating his survey of the audience, and suddenly she realized what he was doing: he was counting the house. He was counting the number of people in the house. And she had great respect for him after that; she could understand that kind of housekeeping.

My mother was a great theatre-goer and both my parents went intermittently to the theatre when I was a young lad. You have to understand that we were very severely lower middle class. One of the reasons I was able to get into the cinema so much was because I knew a lot of the usherettes. I could just tip the wink and scoot in, so my film-going was prodigious. But alas I didn't know the ushers in the theatre in the same kind of way. So the theatre I could most easily afford to go to was the Gate because the Gate had a policy that the last two rows were a shilling, which was cheaper than admission to a cinema if you were forced to pay.

CM: Would the value that people placed upon theatre then be accentuated by the fact that you knew this was not something you could do every week?

JD: Yes, there was a terrific sense of occasion about going to the theatre. You didn't have good duds to wear, but you did the best you could not to destroy it for other people. There was a kind of a sense of decorum.

NG: Did you have a sense of the class of people who were going to the theatre at this time?

JD: Virtually everybody going to the theatre was in my situation; it was a lower-middle-class passion. I can illustrate this. My father's salary was £5 a week, £5 a week, £5 a week. And then there was a big week where he got £7. The big week was the week where you could expect to get a little bit of money. So it was occasionally possible, when the big week came along, to do things you wouldn't otherwise do, like go to the theatre. In terms of socio-economic class, the vast majority of people in the theatre were lower middle class. Even Gabriel Fallon, who was a fairly senior civil servant, might have been getting £6, £6, £6, and £8, but he wasn't getting any more than that. He had a briefcase: that marked him as slightly uppity. And he lived in one of the bigger houses on the Whitworth Road, while we lived in the smaller houses in the cul-de-sacs. But that wasn't a huge divide.

However, in the Dublin of the time, you could not but know about social difference. Right though the 1950s there was an enormous working-class population living right in the centre city. You could not go into Dublin from where I was living without passing through places where coal was sold by the stone, weighed out just as they weighed out potatoes. You have to remember also that during the late 1940s, there were turf mountains in the Phoenix Park. The turf mountains were guarded; and then they were released to the poor, during the winter. And there were an awful lot of poor people. Then there were people like myself and my brother who were occasionally dispatched to the Park in order to create a disturbance and take back a few pieces of turf.

NG: And you the sons of Guards.

JD: Ah yes. My father was very good at turning a blind eye. Sure, he was from North Tipperary and on one side of his family they were all poteen makers. In fact he used to say that a policeman's business was not to arrest all people who committed inappropriate or criminal behaviour. The business of a policeman was to preserve the peace. And sometimes that meant using your head and making a judgement.

CM: Can you give us an idea of what the atmosphere was like for theatregoers like yourself in the 1950s?

JD: You walked home from the theatre, talking in a group. And you were quite passionate about it. I remember when I started going to the Queen's, there was a little platform in the theatre outside the gallery. People used to go out there at the interval and whether they knew each other or not they were all torrentially talking about the play. My impression of the 1950s is best summed up by saying if I went out to the bus stop to get a bus to school or to town on a Monday, people were invariably talking about the Sunday night play.

CM: The Sunday night play on the radio?

JD: Yes. The talk went back and forth: what did you think of it? Was it any good? It was no damned good; it was a bore. They were making all sorts of judgements about it. People talked about the Sunday night play as they talked about plays in the Gate. You have to remember certain things about radio drama at this time. First of all, there was no television. So up to about 1960, when significant numbers of people began to watch television, on Sunday night at 8 o'clock, everything stopped and everybody listened to the play. And they talked about it at the bus stop or school or college the next day.

Now, the plays that were done on Radio Éireann would have included recently performed plays from the Abbey: John McCann, Walter Macken and Donal Giltenan. When they weren't doing such recent plays, they would have put on Synge and O'Casey and T.C. Murray. The radio was gobbling up plays one a week, so there's a huge range of stuff being broadcast. But you also have to remember that BBC radio was coming in, with the Home Service, where they had a repertory company that was doing anything and everything.

I have looked up a record I kept of the plays I heard on radio. In September 1957, for some reason, the Home Service did every play of Terence Rattigan that had been performed, and so I listened to every play of Terence Rattigan. Occasionally there would also be plays by Continental dramatists, Sartre or Ugo Betti. They weren't always very good plays but they were handling interesting themes. Then again, there was another category of play, the play which was written specifically for radio, which couldn't have any other kind of existence, with practitioners like Giles Cooper in England and Padraic Fallon here.

So there were really three different kinds of things. There were things that were happening in the theatre; things that had happened in the theatre and were worth recalling; and then pure radio drama, if there is such a thing.

29

7. "Lady and the Tramp" Feature length cartoon.

11. "Street with No Name" Conventional thriller, Richard Widmark, Mark Stephens, Lyod Naglan.

16. "MARCELINO" [Ladislao Vajda] a religious film which does not break down + weep. Pablito Calvo as a young orphan installed in a monastery. Spain.

March 1. "HIGH NOON" [: Fred Zinnemann for Stanley Kramer => Carl Foreman ʒ Dimitri Tiomkin] One of the v. few great westerns. How an ageing Marshall's support fades as four killers reach a deadline. Gary Cooper, Grace Kelly, Thomas Mitchell, Katy Jurado, Lon Chaney, Lyod Bridges.

11. SHANE [George Stevens ʒ Victor Young => Jack Schaefer ℵ Lyod Griggs] Alan Ladd as the secret, silent hero perforates villainous Jack Palance and rides back whence he came. With Van

Extract from John Devitt's diary dated Speptember 1957

30

"The Little Fugitive" [Raymond Ashley]. 1954.

"The Sign of Venus" [Dino Risi] De Sica, Loren, Sordi.

"12 ANGRY MEN" [Sidney Lumet for Fonda & Rose =>
Reginald Rose & Boris Kaufmann] Trial by Jury. Jack
Warden, Henry Fonda, Martin Balsam, Lee J. Cobb,
Ed Marshall, Ed Begley.

"ROMAN HOLIDAY" [Wm Wyler => Ian MacLellan
Hunter] Audrey Hepburn, Gregory Peck, Eddie Albert. '53.

"The MEDIUM" [Gian Carlo Menotti] Marie Powers
Leo Coleman, Anna Maria Alberghetti.

"LUST FOR LIFE" [Vincente Minelli for John Houseman
Kirk Douglas, Anthony Quinn, Pamela Brown, Jus
Donald. Life of Van Gogh

"The Seventh Sin" [=> Somerset Maugham] El Parker
Geo. Sanders, J.P. Aumont.

"The Rose Tattoo" [Daniel Mann => Tenessee Williams
& James Wong Howe] Serafina (ANNA MAGNANI) With
BURT LANCASTER (ROCCO) With Ben Cooper, Marisa Pavan

CM: And the radio drama, like the theatre, generated talk?

JD: It was a talking town – there was a great oral culture. The continuity with the way Joyce described Dublin in *Ulysses* was very close. I started reading *Ulysses* in the late fifties and it didn't feel like another world. This still felt like the kind of thing that happened when you walked around Dublin. The great paradox about *Ulysses* is that the most bookish of books is also the one where the perfect ear for speech is to be found. There is not one bum note in that book. But more than that, it's the sense of a very crowded town, where people are bumping into each another and they cannot stop talking to each other. And if there's no one to listen, they'll talk to themselves. It was an eager, talkative town.

NG: The fifties are often represented as a grim period of stagnation and repression, but in your account it comes across as a very lively time.

JD: Two things that I think that are very rarely reflected in historical accounts of the fifties. First of all, in the commercial life and business community there was the role of Aer Lingus and the enormous pride it created. I remember one of the Aer Lingus pilots used to walk down the Whitworth Road as I was on my way to

Aer Lingus Advertisement
Circa 1950s

school, and I remember the pride of his walk, and I remember feeling, 'my God, he's doing something for Ireland.' I know now, in these modern times with Aer Lingus in bad repair, this sounds laughable. But it isn't laughable because Aer Lingus was driven by a patriotic fervour and commitment that is really hard now to understand.

The other thing that was very important in Irish life in the 1950s was the GAA. And because of where I lived and because of my father's Tipperary background and enthusiasm for the GAA, I would have been in Croke Park 25 or 30 times a year without fail, from the late forties right through to the late sixties. What was going on there was extraordinary. Even now I notice in listening to commentaries on Radio na Gaeltachta and TG4, when they are talking about hurling in particular, they use an aesthetic language. *Bhí sé sin go hálainn ar fad*; that was extremely beautiful. That was the way that people responded in their tens of thousands to hurling matches at Croke Park: they were dynamic, dramatic occasions.

There was an All-Ireland Final in 1959 where Kilkenny and Waterford played an absolutely extraordinary match which ended in an exact draw, something which is very unusual in hurling because it runs to high scores. My God, you would have wanted to be dead not to be electrified by that match.

So, when we think of the impoverished culture, it's worth remembering that in respect of the kind of hurling that was going on in the fifties, people were not impoverished; they were highly privileged, they knew it, and they described, they felt it; it was an aesthetic experience. And it still is. I know the fifties officially were dull and terrible; emigration was high and all that. But things were happening then – the town was alive with talk. And it was actually not a bad time to be growing up, you know?

Chapter 2
Theatres, Companies and Productions

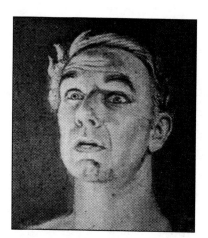

Anew McMaster as Oedipus

CM: We have been talking about your experience of growing up in the 1950s. Anew McMaster's famous touring company was still at work then, wasn't it? Did you ever see them?

JD: Yes, I was lucky enough to see a couple of productions with Anew McMaster in the Gate in the fifties: *Macbeth* was particularly memorable. His voice had developed this tendency to flute and descend – mine is doing it now – but he was wonderful, a terrific actor. Anew McMaster doing those last soliloquies – they can't be done any better than he did them: 'Honour, love, obedience, troops of friends/I must not look to have.' But the problem he had was that people came and went, and he was never able to build up a company. The actor John Molloy told me a wonderful story about acting with McMaster. I ran into John at a one-man show he was doing in Balbriggan; it was very good, about his own life, growing up with T.B. and then having a career on the stage. Afterwards I met him having a drink at the bar, told him how much I enjoyed the show, and asked him what it was like when he became an actor. And he told me this story which he had foolishly decided not to include in his one-man show.

McMaster's company was playing *Lear* somewhere in the southwest – maybe Dingle, maybe Tralee – in a Muintir na Tíre hall that was badly equipped. There was no way you could get in backstage from outside; the only way you could get backstage was through the auditorium. This was a serious drawback. So McMaster insisted that they all come along to the theatre with overcoats, dressed for the part, and that they wait behind the curtain until the audience came in. So they had to go there an hour before the bloody play was due to start. And then he insisted at the end that nobody was to leave the theatre until the last member of the audience had gone. So they took their curtain, they put on their overcoats, and they waited. But of course there was one guy who didn't go – sitting in an

35

aisle seat, an old geezer, with his hands on his walking stick. They were looking at their watches: Jesus, *Lear* is a long, thirsty play. They wanted to make a break for a drink. So they asked McMaster: could they leave? Oh, no. They asked him again: no, no. Eventually: yes, yes, we can go. So they all marched down the steps in front of the stage, down the auditorium, down the centre aisle, and when they got to the bloke, he stood up, and he reached over to McMaster, and he grabbed him by the hand, and shook him by the hand, and he said: 'That was wonderful. Tell me, which one of ye wrote it?'

NG: It's a wonderful story. Earlier you stressed the importance of radio drama at this time. Radio Éireann still had its own company of actors at this stage, didn't they?

JD: They were really something special. I don't know how many of their recordings survive, but the actors in that company – Thomas Studley, George Greene, Seamus Forde, Ginette Waddell, Daphne Carroll, Brendan Cauldwell – they were really prodigiously gifted. It was such a delight because no matter how large the cast was, you never lost your way in a play because the voices were all crystal clear and sharply discriminated. The most remarkable voice I have ever heard anywhere is Thomas Studley's. Listen to any of the performances of Thomas Studley and you will have no doubt whatever about the truth of what I am saying: a wonderful actor with a cut glass voice.

NG: Was there any particular theatre production that for you caught the spirit of the fifties?

JD: *The Crucible: The Crucible* was terrific to see in the fifties. I saw it in the summer of 1959 in the Olympia, with Barry Cassin in the lead. And I knew it was about the McCarthy business, and I thought: 'wow, this is up-to-date stuff!' But it wasn't just its topicality at the time. Every time I've seen it since, even though we're further and further away from the

McCarthy period, the play has become more interesting. And the reason it has become more interesting is that Miller has really worried about getting Salem right: making the economic question, the question of land, the question of authority, and the question of religion in that community richly significant. He has devoted a huge amount of imaginative energy to inventing a world, in which political questions surface. Salem is in transition. It's moving from being one kind of society to another kind of society, and it's not able to cope with that process of its own transition.

The Queen's Theatre

CM: This was the period of the Abbey's long exile at the Queen's, which most people think of as a low point in the theatre's history.

JD: It was a difficult time for them. They didn't know how long they were to be at the Queen's; they were there for fifteen years, from 1951 to 1966, and they thought they were going to be there for two or three years. So, there was a kind play-safe policy to start with and then a kind of despair. Because they never expected to be so long in the Queen's, after the first couple of years they didn't spend any money on the theatre. It was ready to fall to pieces. They didn't renew the fabric – I remember the disgusting condition of the seats. There's a story of Ray McAnally that will tell you something about the physical condition of the Queen's. McAnally told me a wonderful story about playing the part of Columba there in Brian Friel's play *The Enemy Within*. He is sitting there with his great monk's skirts, and the next thing a drop falls on his skirt: there's a leak in the ceiling. He's in a really serious situation: he's giving out the lines, but it looks to all the world that he's wet himself.

CM: What was the stage of the Queen's like?

JD: I think it was very good. You could do naturalist drama in a box set without apology, like for example, *Long Day's Journey into Night*; there was no difficulty, it didn't loom too large. At the same time, you could do very adventurous, free-moving things, like pantos and Brecht's *Galileo*. There was a terrific

---

ABBEY THEATRE
— DUBLIN —

Playing at
THE QUEEN'S THEATRE
Pending Rebuilding and Enlargement of the Abbey

Tuesday, 28th April, 1959 and following evenings at 6.30

First Irish Production of

LONG DAY'S JOURNEY INTO NIGHT
A Play in Four Acts by Eugene O'Neill

Characters :

JAMES TYRONE	Pilib O Floinn
MARY CAVAN TYRONE	Ria Mooney
JAMES TYRONE, JR., their elder son	Tomás P. MacCionaith
EDMUND TYRONE, their younger son	Uinsionn O Dubhláinn
CATHLEEN, a maid servant	Caitlín Ní Bhearáin- Kathleen Barror

ACT I: Living room of the Tyrone's summer home 8.30 a.m. on a day in August, 1912.

ACT II, Scene I: The same, around 12.45 p.m.
Scene II: The same, about a half hour later.

ACT III: The same, around 6.30 that evening.

ACT IV: The same, around midnight.

SMOKING WILL NOT BE PERMITTED IN THE AUDITORIUM

energy and drive in those productions. And it was acoustically superb. I don't know why it is that theatres built long ago are superior acoustically and visually to more recent theatres. Acoustics is a very weird science. Another good thing about the Queen's was that there were plenty of places where you could go and talk in the interval or afterwards. I mentioned the platform outside the gods before, but there was plenty of space downstairs as well. So the Queen's had a number of advantages: social, theatrical and acoustic.

CM: Was there a sense that people saw those advantages, or was there a sense that this was just marking time?

JD: Yes, there was a sense of marking time. I think people became retrospectively aware of these things.

NG: Was there one play from the time at the Queen's that stands out for you?

JD: *Long Day's Journey into Night* was staged in the Queen's: that's the performance that I think I go back to mentally most often. Any chance I had of a normal life went when I saw that production. You keep on going back in the hope of seeing something like that.

CM: What was it that made that production stand out so much?

JD: It was the way that the family in that play came together. All the actors were uncannily brilliant. But much more than that, it was like watching a team of people who were really *au fait* with what they were doing. I read recently in Vincent Dowling's autobiography, where he talks about the rehearsal period of that play. They had an unusually long rehearsal period, and they used to wander off into a pub and rehearse a scene there, then have a drink and return to the rehearsal room and rehearse it again. They were the family.

There was a weird thing about that play. It's haunted by notions of Catholic religion, grace, redemption, and yet it's a play in which God does not appear. And that summed up the way a lot of people felt about the world at the time. Many people, like myself, would have had a sacramental view of Christianity and of the world, but also a nagging suspicion that maybe there was no God after all. That's the riven character of the play. And at the same time, there was the visible fact that this family, who all loved each other, they were tearing each other apart, or when they weren't tearing each other apart, were tearing themselves apart.

T.P. McKenna played Jamie, which is a very difficult part for an actor because it's not very well written, compared to the other parts. You have to be as good as T.P. McKenna to bring it off. In the last act there's a terrifying scene where he pours out his life to his brother, and asks for forgiveness and tells him: look, I'm going to be out to destroy you because that's the kind of person I am.

NG: And the give-away line about 'I hate your guts kid.' It's extraordinary.

JD: And telling you this proves it.

CM: Who directed that production? Was it Tomás Mac Anna or Frank Dermody?

JD: Frank Dermody. I know people who saw Dermody directing, and they said that the uncanny thing about him in rehearsal was that when he was showing moves to women, he was a woman. He was apparently a wonderful actor, but he wasn't the full shilling. The

Frank Dermody

brutal fact of the matter is that he had a very serious drink problem.

I'll tell you one story about Frank Dermody. I met him in a bar – the Prince's Bar, just beside the Capitol Cinema, more or less where BHS shop is now – and discovered who he was. He was sitting on a bar stool and he was pretty legless by this stage. I was talking to him about productions he had done, particularly *Long Day's Journey into Night*. He said: 'yeah, yeah, yeah, great play, great play, great play. Don't cut it, don't cut it, don't cut it.' He said everything three times. Then I happened to mention Micheál Mac Líammóir by name. At which, he got off the stool, he got hold of the stool, and he volunteered to feck it at me. There was no question of his hitting me with the bar stool. I mean, he would have liked to have done so, he wanted to do so, but he lacked the power to do so.

I was very puzzled by this at the time, but I found a possible explanation, years later, reading the text of *Diarmaid agus Gráinne*, the Irish language play Mac Líammóir wrote for the opening of the Taibhdhearc Theatre. Looking at the cast list at the back, I discovered that Proinsias Mac Diarmaidadh was one of the actors in a small part. So, whatever the hell prompted him to offer to strike me with a bar stool at the mention of Mac Líammóir's name, may have had its roots way back. At least Dermody evidently knew Mac Líammóir from the time he started in the Taibhdhearc.

NG: Apart from Dermody, Tomás Mac Anna would have been the other notable Abbey director at the time. How far were you aware of him as a director?

JD: I was very aware of him, particularly for his ability to handle crowds: I don't think he was terribly good at intimate exchanges. He was very lucky in that he got to direct the Irish language pantomimes, and that gave him a kind of freedom that he wouldn't have had if he was doing plays in box sets, which had rational plots and predictable resolutions. In the *geamaireacht* there was no narrative logic that I ever discerned, and anything could happen and usually did. They were the direct antithesis of everything else that was going on in the theatre, that kind of dreary naturalism. It was a kind of bank holiday. It was possible because it was in Irish, and therefore you couldn't criticize it.

CM: Were there particular productions of Mac Anna that you remember?

JD: His production of *Galileo* was terrifically exciting. It was a physically exciting performance, with the swirl of the crowds coming on. You knew it had been rehearsed, but it didn't feel like that: he got that rough, edgy quality. He had a way of breaking up the production, so that you were taken away on a wave and then you were suddenly shocked and stopped still. I thought it was terrific, and I tried a reduced production with the students at Glenstall Abbey, when I was teaching there. And it worked quite nicely. It isn't a play that requires wonderful actors with great inwardness. It is a play that requires actors who are shameless, fearless, and I had plenty of those.

NG: And other outstanding plays Mac Anna directed?

JD: There was the production of Lorca's *Yerma* at the Queen's, which was all lemon and yellow and red: that was Mac

Tomás Mac Anna

42

Anna's. That was really startling to look at. I don't think I understood the play but there was a visual aspect to the production that was absolutely unprecedented in anything I'd seen before. I had never seen anybody who wanted to marry movement and light and colour in the way Mac Anna was doing in that production.

CM: So there were highlights even in the Abbey's down time at the Queen's. And there was the Gate ...

JD: Going to the Gate at that time was absolutely terrific. You could get in very cheaply; you didn't have to dress up; Lord Longford would be collecting for the theatre at the door and if you put a penny in his box, he'd give you a big smile, and by God, he was a big man, it was a really big smile. Longford had the theatre for half the year, and another company for six months. Longford would do *The Good-Natured Man*, that kind of refined 18th-century stuff. And then there would be somebody coming in doing Ibsen, there was a lot of Ibsen done there.

    Eve Watkinson was absolutely superb in a production of *Hedda Gabler*. That show produced

ABBEY THEATRE

Proprietors	THE NATIONAL THEATRE SOCIETY
Directors	ERNEST BLYTHE, ROIBEARD O'FARACHAIN,
	SEAMUS DE BHILMOT, GABRIEL FALLON
	WALTER MACKEN
Secretary	ERIC GORMAN

MONDAY, 28TH FEBRUARY 1966
AND FOLLOWING NIGHTS AT 8

YERMA
A TRAGIC POEM IN THREE ACTS
by FREDERICO GARCIA LORCA
in the translation of James Graham-Lujan and Richard O'Connell

HALL OF HEALING
A PLAY IN ONE ACT
by SEAN O'CASEY

LATECOMERS NOT ADMITTED UNTIL END OF FIRST ACT

STALLS 10/- & 8/-.; DRESS CIRCLE 10/- & 8/-.:
UPPER CIRCLE 5/-; GALLERY 2/6

BOOKING AT QUEENS THEATRE
BOX OFFICE OPEN 10.30 TO 6.   'PHONE 44505

Corrigan & Wilson, Ltd., Dublin

a crisis in the Gate. My father was stationed in Store Street Garda Station at the time, and the Gate rang to report the theft of the duelling pistols from *Hedda Gabler*. How was she going to shoot herself? It was a danger and difficulty. There was a flyboy Guard, who was looking for promotion and he insisted that the IRA had to be prime suspects because the '57-'62 border campaign had just started. So my father had to go along with the flyboy to the theatre to investigate the possibility that the IRA had stolen the duelling pistols in order to attack a police station. It helps to fix the date of the production.

I would have seen literally everything that was done in the Gate in the late fifties. In retrospect they weren't often the best productions but you were bloody glad to be seeing Goldsmith and Ibsen, plays that you wouldn't have had a snowball's chance in hell of seeing in the Queen's. In that sense, they were doing a great service. It was a kind of education to know that there were plays in the 18th century and that they could still be done.

NG: Were Edwards and Mac Líammóir not playing in the Gate then?

JD: No, they didn't play in the Gate, but they did play in the Gaiety. In the period that I'm talking about, 1956 to 1960, I'm

Lord Longford collecting donations for the Gate

pretty certain Edwards and Mac Líammóir did not play in the Gate.

CM: Then the sense of the Gate in those years would have been that it was Longford's theatre rather than Edwards and Mac Líammóir's.

JD: Yes. I was born just that agonizing moment too late to see them in their heyday. I saw them in the late fifties and early sixties occasionally, when they were often sneered at. They used to say about Hilton Edwards. 'He's not a theatre director at all, he's a lighting technician.' Or Mac Líammóir was just a ham. Dublin was a town that liked celebrating theatre but it also loved cutting people down to size. There's a kind of edge to the Dublin wit. Cut him down, I remember him when he had no backside in his trousers.

NG: 'Tis far from it he was reared.

JD: Exactly, that's the one.

NG: But did Edwards's skills in lighting and Mac Líammóir's in design make a real difference to their productions? Is there any one show you remember for its visual effects?

JD: There was the production of *The Informer*, which I think would be about 1958 in the Olympia. That was like looking at a German Expressionist movie, the stage looked utterly different. That was probably a fairly consistent feature of the Mac Líammóir-Edwards school.

45

In that production, they seemed to be communicating not just the atmosphere of the 1920s but also the mood of the piece through the costumes and the appearance of the stage, which I think was a trick of lighting as well as stage design.

CM: Were there other talented directors besides Edwards himself who worked for the company?

JD: Jim Fitzgerald. He was a remarkable actor and a wonderful director. He directed a hell of a lot of plays in the Gate, and they were as smooth as shot silk, really well done. He became an alcoholic and wrecked himself, but for about ten years, from about the mid-fifties to the mid-sixties, he was an absolutely outstanding director. I believe he directed *Stephen D*, for instance, Hugh Leonard's theatrical adaptation at the Gate. He was highly respected, and when there were little talk shops associated with the theatre festival, Fitzgerald would frequently speak at them.

NG: I remember him myself very vividly indeed because I was in a terrible show in a student drama festival in 1966, where he was the adjudicator, and he tore strips off us. I still remember standing in the wings, listening to this total excoriation. Quite rightly so, but oh my God, I'll never forget that man's face.

Poster for Abbey Production of *Stephen D*.
Dir. Joe Dowling

JD: Yes, he had very pointed features, hatchet-faced you might say.

NG: And rather red-faced.

JD: That happens with alcoholics. They look vaguely human for a time until a point is reached where all their features grow very sharp, and they no longer observe the ordinary courtesies. They're just too obsessive about the next drink. But he had very high standards, as your story illustrates. By 1966 I think he was more or less a spent force as a director, but he was certainly remarkable in his time.

CM: We've talked about the Abbey at the Queen's and the Gate with its various companies. Were there other smaller theatres operating at this time that you remember? Did you see anything of the Gas Company?

JD: Yes, I went out to Dún Laoghaire to see Pinter's *The Caretaker*. Oh, it was a wicked place, it was terrible: my God almighty, to travel that distance to see a play and to be so uncomfortable. It was very limited in what it could do. You could only do that kind of play, with three people sitting around and shouting at each other and insulting each other and relieving their disturbances.

NG: When I saw them, they were up somewhere in Parnell Square, in a little basement.

JD: Ah! That's the place where they did *The Little Hut*. That's an interesting case. It's a kind of sexy play, set on a desert island, with people getting up to no good in it, in a sexual sense: it was filmed in the late fifties, with Ava Gardner. That play ran literally for years, two or three years, in that tiny basement theatre on Parnell Square, almost opposite Findlater's church.

NG: What I saw there was the Shelagh Delaney play *A Taste of Honey*, which also ran and ran.

JD: People's tongues were hanging out for irregular sex in plays because there were such constraints on behaviour.

NG: What about *The Rose Tattoo* at the Pike in 1957?

JD: Oh, that was hilarious. My father knew the Guard who gave the testimony, and he went to see my da for advice because he knew that my da went to the theatre a lot. The poor Guard was frigid with embarrassment. 'One of them things, you know.' That was the contraceptive. He didn't know whether he saw it or not.

NG: You couldn't confess that you'd even recognize one.

JD: 'But Christ, Jack', he said to my father, 'what will I say, what will I do?' Yes, that was an ugly case. And what was ugly about that was that it damaged the marriage and the lives of Alan Simpson and Carolyn Swift. But it also had its ludicrous, comic side.

NG: Did you go to the Pike much?

JD: No, I didn't go the Pike at all because no sooner was I interested in the Pike than it was gone. But later on, when I was already teaching down in Glenstal, I used to go to the Focus – that's a theatre we've rather forgotten about. The Focus was really important: they did a lot of stuff off the beaten track that definitely wasn't going to be performed in the major theatre. They did O'Neill's *Mourning Becomes Electra*, for example; you need a big appetite to do *Mourning Becomes Electra*. And they did The *Iceman Cometh*. They did productions of Chekhov; they did productions of Ibsen; they did some later productions of the American dramatists, like Clifford Odets. They were not at all afraid of the intensities of these plays in that tiny theatre. It's lovely to be that intimate with actors: you can't beat that feeling that you're sitting in their laps.

The Focus had a tiny clientele, but it was solid. The American actor Ozzy Whitehead used to turn up, and he'd be sitting outside reminiscing about productions in the 1930s on Broadway. He was very old, pushing the hundred mark the last time I spoke to him. And he was still on about Maxwell Anderson's *Winterset*: I think he played in the original production in 1935. 'Ah, what a great play it was, and nobody would do it any more. And maybe the Focus would do it.' But at that stage he was so old, he was only able for an hour at a time.

The Focus Theatre in 2007

I remember coming up from Limerick to see something in the Focus on a Saturday night and then being told that on the Sunday night they were going to do improvs. So I stayed over to see the improvs, and they were absolutely staggering. The result was that I had to drive down to work about three hours later having had a couple of hours sleep. It isn't that easy, if you leave the Focus about half eleven or twelve at night to get home, to get a bit of sleep, and then go on to work.

The Focus was terrifically important because it produced new actors like Tom Hickey and very high standards of production. When they did plays like *A View from the Bridge*, the theatre might be all wrong: it was much too small. But that didn't really matter because the intensity and passion of the plays were respected.

CM: What about amateur companies?

JD: At one stage I don't think you could have delivered coal in the centre of the city without burying an amateur company. There was a crowd in Merrion Square, the Lantern.

NG: Oh, I remember the Lantern.

JD: Yes? They did some queer stuff, but they did things very badly, though. The cruel thing about theatre is that, if you see a great production, or you are used at least to very efficient production of worthwhile plays, and then you see rather bad productions, it's awful:

Poster for a Peacock production of *Happy Days* featuring O.Z. Whitehead

suffering of a kind that only the damned have to endure. There was a guy living on our road who was a member of the Lantern company, so I used to go along out of solidarity. But I used to suffer. I remember once they did the *Bacchae*.

NG: Oh dear Lord, in the Lantern?

JD: You think that's bad, wait till I tell you. They did it on a series of camp beds, so they could have people at different levels on the camp beds. That's how they did the *Bacchae*. Need I say more?

CM: But they weren't all bad, the amateur companies, were they?

JD: No, indeed. The best production of *The Plough and the Stars* I ever saw was done when the play was banned by O'Casey. It was done by a group called Cairde Fáil, which was a Fianna Fáil ensemble, in the Queen's. They only got in because they were an amateur company; the O'Casey ban applied only to professional stage productions. They rehearsed for months as a company entirely devoted to the play, and with a feeling for the play. The result was terrific, catching the way the play shifts gear and uses different technical means in each act, and generalizes itself superbly at the end. It's an absolutely wonderful play, but if it has a weakness, it's in the love scenes. There again, though, in that Cairde Fáil production the young lovers were innocent and naïve, and maybe you can get away with the love scenes, if moon-faced stricken creatures play it, as they did.

CM: What do you feel was the general importance of the amateur theatre movement?

JD: It was trying to create some sort of mirror image of what it's like to be human and live in the social world – a mirror is probably the wrong word, but let it stand for the moment. And they didn't have theatres. One of the things that is really interesting about the amateur dramatic movement is where they put on shows. They put them on in Muintir na Tíre halls in towns and villages around the country, or parish halls, the windy places that couldn't be heated and didn't have proper ventilation. They played under enormous restraints and part of the sheer joy came from overcoming the restrictions and resistance of the venues.

NG: The new Abbey building was a long time coming. Were there reasons for the delay that you know of?

JD: They were having difficulty over the site. Right next door to the old Abbey was a pub and the pub owner was holding out for a fortune. You've heard the story?

NG: No.

JD: The story is that Ernest Blythe was losing his rag over this. He was getting very, very impatient. So he called in some actors, and he said to them: 'You guys act for a living. Well, I want you to go along into the pub and give the performance of your life. You're to talk about the new plan, which doesn't require buying the pub, and how it's going to be the most splendid theatre in Europe. You dish out the pay to that publican, and make sure he believes you.' So, three or four of the senior company – I think the two Goldens were involved – went in to the pub and started shooting the breeze, talking about the wonderful fact that they were going to come back to this place, and they didn't need the pub. The pub would be handy for the playgoers; they could hop out and get a drink. And the pub owner went into a flat spin of panic, and he sold as soon as he could. But one of the reasons for the delay was he would not sell.

CM: I heard the story from an architectural source. But the spin I heard on it was that Michael Scott was involved in this as well. He allegedly drew up a set of cod plans for an L-shaped building that went around the pub.

JD: There's no doubt about it, the pub owner was conned. So the theatre came into existence, for better or worse. In fact, I don't like the present Abbey Theatre. It was a missed opportunity. Although Michael Scott was a great theatre man, and he no doubt had some theory to justify what he was doing, I don't think the result was happy. It's not acoustically good, and it's inhospitable to the Abbey Theatre's own classics. I remember a grotesque production of *Riders to the Sea* in which they had the full cottage on stage. Do you remember that one?

NG: Yes, I do.

JD: Remember the cloudscapes behind. Oh, Jesus! Excuse me, but it was a bit much. And they had to do it like that because of the size of the stage, the Cinemascope vision. It is strange that they created in the 1960s a theatre space which is not hospitable to Synge, O'Casey, or any of the naturalistic plays.

NG: For Synge it's got to be an enclosed space: you can't do anything else with it. And the same with O'Casey.

JD: Yes, it's true. You can have the outside of the tenements, but you don't need it. As a matter of fact, the surplus space gets in the way of the play. These are very tightly constructed plays, and they are really about people confronting each other in a narrow space. So when you change the space, you change the dynamic and you also change the relationship between the audience and the stage. There's an acoustic dead spot in the Abbey, if you go to the right-hand side. I happened once to go to the right-hand side about three or four rows back to see a production of *The Plough and the Stars*: if I hadn't known the play by heart, I would have only heard every second or third line. It's a completely dead area.

CM: It does work for some plays, though, doesn't it?

JD: Certainly. It worked for Louis MacNeice's *One for the Grave* in 1956 – I thought that was a dazzling production. Now, maybe I was just besotted; you have to remember that I am seriously besotted with the theatre. No doubt there were a lot of things wrong with *One for the Grave*, but I thought it was amazing. It was the first proper play done in the new Abbey. There were celebrations of the Abbey: the Abbey looks back, the Abbey looks into its navel. There were various sorts of self-congratulatory, important things I could not be bothered going to. I knew there was going to be no play there, and what I wanted was a play.

CM: When the new Abbey opened, was there a sense of there being a lot more resources to do things like design?

JD: Yes, I think that's absolutely true. There was a friend of mine, a very distinguished painter called John Kelly. He was much struck by the fact that the Abbey actually invited people in to design decent playbills, which they had never had before. John designed about 20 or 30 playbills for them. He was himself an interesting playwright and wrote a play, staged in 1961, with a resurrection motif in it called *The Third Day*. The central part, a character named Ned Doyle, was written for John Molloy, the wonderful actor who played in Tom Kilroy's *Talbot's Box*. I've often wondered if Kilroy had seen that play – it was done in the Gate.

CM: The new Abbey gave the National Theatre a fresh impetus, but there were alternative theatrical spaces opening in the 1970s as well, such as the Project. How important was that?

JD: The Project moved around a lot, you know. When I went to see them first, they were in a basement in Middle Abbey Street. Then they were in a weird warehouse across the road from the Gaiety. And then they went to an equally weird warehouse on the site of the present theatre. They did all sorts of things, but the fact that they were working in that kind of space meant that they had to reconceive even naturalistic productions.

CM: What would be the earliest thing you remember in the Project?

JD: It was that mad play about the rehearsal in the looney bin of de Sade.

NG: *Marat Sade*.

JD: *Marat Sade*: they did that in a basement in Middle Abbey Street. Then there was a very interesting production of the *Antigone* of Anouilh in the warehouse opposite the Gaiety. I don't know who directed it, but it was a terrific production: brave and deliberate. It was this idea of a space which hadn't been sanctified but was now sanctified.

I'll tell you one thing I noticed in the Project. I went one day with the wife, and we didn't go out for some reason at the break; there were too many people in the theatre and we weren't going to get a cup of coffee anyway so we stayed there. And I noticed something very interesting. Even in the Project in East Essex Street, when people were going to the loo, which was virtually backstage, they walked around the unmarked stage space, as if it was an altar space. Isn't that really extraordinary? It's as if there was some sort of vestigial religious reverence there, in spite of the wealth and confidence of the new state and all the rest of it.

NG: There was a new generation in the Abbey at this time also, wasn't there, with the coming of Joe Dowling, for instance?

JD: Yes. Can I tell you a funny story about Dowling? This is an absolutely true story about Dowling and Mac Anna. I went to a terrifically Brechtian production of *The Plebeians Rehearse the Uprising* by Günter Grass and Ralph Manheim in the Peacock. I knew Mac Anna to see – I had seen him around the town – and it became glaring that Joe Dowling had modelled his walk and his gestures and everything on Mac Anna. Now, there was a huge age difference: Dowling would have been maybe 22 or 23 at the time, and Mac Anna must have been 50 plus. It was an afternoon performance, and I went into the bar afterwards and got talking to Mac Anna. I said: what do you think of this young guy Dowling? He said: Dowling is wonderful; Dowling is x, y, and z, and what's more, he's a, b, and c; he was thrilled with Dowling. And I said: yes, and he does a terrific take-off of you, doesn't he? I assumed he knew. But he hadn't a clue – it had never dawned on him – even though he did have the most striking walk. Tomás Mac Anna had a walk you would recognize at 500 yards. If he was coming towards you on the Great North Road, you'd know him at half a mile. The top of his body looked like a coat hanger, and he had a way of leaning forward when he walked and barking when he talked. He barked – it was just the way he talked. It made it glaringly obvious that Dowling's performance was a quite minutely observed take-off by this mischievous young actor. But Mac Anna couldn't see it. Satire is a mirror in which the reader sees everyone's face but his own.

CM: The Peacock did provide a space for different, more experimental shows, didn't it? I'm thinking of those productions that Patrick Mason did with Tom Mac Intyre and Tom Hickey in the eighties.

JD: The production of *The Great Hunger* was the high point of that series. There were other things that were very good, but that was superb. I remember going back cheerfully with my two very young kids to that; they were six and eight at the time. It was such terrific fun to see the stage used like that, with the lack of embarrassment about the human body and its absurdities and its functions.

NG: Hickey hanging upside down on the gate.

JD: The old mother as a wooden object and the wonderful neighing horses. I think I saw it four times, and enjoyed it hugely on every occasion. Mac Intyre also did an interesting Swift play, *The Bearded Lady*. Something very funny happened during the production of that play. It's very clear that Conrad in *Heart of Darkness* picked up on the last chapter of *Gulliver's Travels*, where they talk about the myths of origins of the Yahoos, and discuss the proposal whether or not they should exterminate the brutes. But it is also clear that Mac Intyre fed that back into his Swift play. In other words, he allowed Swift to be influenced by one of

57

Swift's successors. There was a discussion after the play where it became apparent that Patrick Mason didn't know that, and the reason Mason didn't know is that Mac Intyre had deliberately kept him in the dark. It came up in the discussion, and Mason realized that something was going on. I remember his head jerking around: 'Mac Intyre, what is this?' And Mac Intyre said: 'oh well, we didn't go into that at the time. It worked out very well.' It raises the question: how much does the director need to know? And the answer is that he doesn't need to know everything to do the job properly.

Chapter 3
Performers and Performances

Vincent Dowling and T.P. McKenna in 1959 Abbey Production of
Long Day's Journey into Night

CM: One of the difficult things in talking about actors, it seems to me, is a paucity of vocabulary. Somebody like Ria Mooney, for instance, whose performance in *Long Day's Journey* you so much admired: what was it about Ria Mooney that would have made her so impressive on stage?

JD: Well, there are scenes in that play where she doesn't have to dominate, and there are scenes where she has to dominate without any assertion. In the last scene, she cannot be assertive. She has to be just precise. She has to have absolute precision and utter trust in the material that she is handling: the adequacy of the language and whatever direction she is receiving. Precision, vocal adequacy, physical competence, the ability to be unobtrusive, but also, vulnerability – that's something an actor needs as well. I saw that when I reviewed Des Cave's performance in *Childish Things*. Do you know that play?

It's a play by Sean McCarthy, about a bloke who comes back to live in Cork, and is being fractured trying to make his marriage work and find an economic basis for it. I thought it was excellent: maybe not a great play, but one that said something about what was actually going on in Ireland at that time, and what was likely to happen in the immediate future. Des Cave gave an absolutely superb performance in that. The character has to come apart at the seams, and it's very difficult for an actor to do that. First of all, you have to have the build-up of the character and then the disintegration. And there's nowhere you can go wrong, because if you do go wrong, the whole thing is phoney and it's useless. Anyway I reviewed that production, and I wrote to Des Cave about it. When I met him, I was horribly embarrassed because he was so grateful. 'But why are you grateful to me?', I said. 'For God's sake, you've given one of the great performances that I've seen; I'm your debtor.' 'Ah, God no', he said. 'It's great to hear this. I really worked at that'. Actors in general are riddled with doubt. They're very tough on themselves, and much given to despair.

NG: Presumably it is part of the territory in so far as you're out there putting yourself on the line every night. Training and technique, though, must also be crucial parts of the achievement, don't you think?

JD: Absolutely. Gabriel Fallon told me that it took F.J. McCormick about an hour and a half before the production to be right. If you went near him during that hour and a half, you would regret it – he wasn't hospitable to interruptions. He was getting focussed. I never saw him on the stage; of course, we've all seen him in film. But that intensity that he had was down to the labour he put into it. It's a bit like a teacher who prepares scrupulously, goes in and gives a blinding class, and one of his pupils comes up afterwards and says: 'God, that was spontaneous and wonderful.' And of course, the whole thing has been entirely sweated out.

CM: How much is individual talent and how much is learned from other actors?

JD: Learning from others is crucially important. The early Abbey was a repertory company; they were highly disciplined and mutually supportive on the stage. In repertory people are

Des Cave in 2003 Abbey production of *She Stoops to Conquer.*

61

learning from each other, and if they're playing big parts and small parts alternately, they're learning more about the theatre than they could possibly learn any other way. It's a long apprenticeship. I mean, when did Donal McCann emerge as a great actor? That wasn't immediately obvious. How much did McCann owe to playing in the Abbey repertory? True, he had experience in television in England in the sixties, and he was an embryonic genius, but it was quite late in the day that people realized that this guy is really exceptional. It was those scenes in *Faith Healer*, where he became conscious of power. I remember him holding his hand like that to the audience – 'I've got you. I've got you' – followed by an incredibly long pause and nobody breathing. At that point, McCann was fully conscious of his power. But it might have taken him twenty years to get that good. Cyril Cusack hadn't the name for being generous to other actors but he was amazed at McCann in the part. 'I've been going back night after night,' he told me. 'I want to see how he does it: it's the most amazing performance I've ever seen.' This was not Cyril Cusack's usual idiom.

Donal McCann in 1980 Abbey Production of *Faith Healer*.

CM: Not the most generous of actors, Cusack, but a great performer himself, did you think?

JD: Indeed he was. I would guess it was in 1957, when I would have been about 16, that I saw Cyril Cusack play Hamlet in the Gaiety. And that was really, really interesting.

NG: His own company, wasn't it?

JD: Yes, and it was an extraordinary cast, because do you know who Claudius was? Mac Líammóir. Mac Líammóir was not up to playing Hamlet anymore, but he was a terrific Claudius. Denis Brennan was Horatio, and Coralie Carmichael was Gertrude. They played the whole thing, it took four hours and a bit, they just did everything. Cusack played Hamlet as a man of extraordinary bottled up energy. In Act III, Scene I, the prayer scene with Ophelia, I remember vividly he'd shoot off the stage when he said something he was satisfied with, and then he'd shoot on again. 'God hath given you one face and you give yourselves another.' And he'd go off and think of something else. The energy with which he bounced on and off was extraordinary. The idea that Hamlet was some sort of effete fop adjusting himself in front of a mirror never crossed my mind. Hamlet to me is Cyril Cusack. I don't know if you've read or heard anything about that performance, but it was superb.

Cyril Cusack in 1963

NG: Well, this is an occasion to give you my reminiscence, John. Cyril Cusack was a mate of my father's and I remember him coming and visiting us, down in Wicklow where I still live, and walking up the hill behind our house memorizing the lines for *Hamlet*. I didn't see the production, of course, because I was only nine or ten at the time, but it was my first image of an actor, this man taking himself off and walking up and down the country road, learning off the lines of *Hamlet*.

JD: Well, he knew them. It was an amazing performance. I've seen dozens of Hamlets since, but they all seemed wrong to me. I suppose the first performance does to some degree define the way you understand the part. But I think Cusack was right; in his Hamlet there was venom, there was energy, there was attack, there was something to sit on. If Hamlet achieves leisure for reflection, he does so occasionally and he does so by keeping something down.

NG: That was one of Cusack's extraordinary strengths, wasn't it, the capacity to release energy at a particular point? Later on he underplayed all the time but he could still turn on a surge at certain moments.

JD: He was pacing himself I think too. I remember his Shylock in the Abbey, where it was very clear that he was just reciting, and then suddenly he was really present.

CM: You mentioned Micheál Mac Líammóir playing Claudius to Cusack's Hamlet. He too must have been one of the great theatrical figures of your time.

JD: The first time I saw him play a theatrical lead was as Gypo Nolan in *The Informer* in 1958. At that stage, I was an outstanding film buff. I was absolutely intolerable: on every film, I wanted to know who directed it and who played every part in it and what else they did. Anyway, *The Informer* was revived and it was shown in the Astor on the quays. And I went along and Victor McLaglen's performance was amazing. The next thing I open the paper: *The Informer* with Micheál Mac Líammóir is going to be done at the Olympia! Previous to this, I had seen Mac Líammóir as Claudius, and I had seen him in pantos at the Gaiety with Jimmy O'Dea, doing little one-act sketches based on Edgar Allen Poe's 'The Cask of Amontillado', that kind of stuff. And I knew he was of below average height and that he didn't have massive bulk of the kind that Victor McLaglen had. So I thought to myself: Jesus, this is incredible. I mean, how's he going to play Gypo Nolan? I went along and five minutes into the performance, I had completely forgotten; he was bloody wonderful. He was obviously wearing lifts and had padded his jacket, but I didn't notice that at the time. The fact of the matter is that he was entirely credible.

Orson Welles as Falstaff in *Chimes at Midnight*.

CM: He is famous of course for his Iago in the Orson Welles film of *Othello*. Did he ever play it on stage?

65

JD: Indeed he did. By the way, I also saw Welles in Dublin on stage.

CM: Oh, did you?

JD: Yes, he played in the Gaiety. Now, when was this? I was in first year, so it was either late 1959 or early 1960, and he played Falstaff. He was essentially playing the part he filmed so well in *Chimes at Midnight*. I think he had Norman Rodway in the film and in the play, but it was difficult to know who was on stage with Orson because Orson tended to absorb all the light. You know the famous line, in *The Player*, the play about the actor-manager, where the actor-manager says: you can switch on that light and it will hit me here, and you can switch on that light and it will hit me there. And the lighting man says: so what about the others? 'They must find what light they can.' That was Orson.

But to go back to the stage *Othello*, where Mac Líammóir played Iago, it was in the theatre festival in 1962 in the Gaiety. I went along on a Wednesday afternoon to see the matinée performance and Mac Líammóir was so damn good, that I hid in the loo, and I came out and saw it again that evening. I'm not bullshitting you: this is absolutely true. You could do that in those days because you didn't have to go into a seat; you could still stand at the back. So it was perfectly possible. I got in in the afternoon for 2/6, standing. I didn't have a sausage left, and I hadn't eaten anything, but damn it all, that performance of *Othello* was really incandescent. To sit through a play twice in the same day, or rather to stand through a play twice on the same day, is not something that I would recommend. But in that particular case it was worth it.

NG: And who was playing opposite him, do you remember?

JD: The Othello was a film actor called William Marshall, and he was superlative. These were two performances, one given by a Martian and the other given by a Venusian, with planetary differences between the styles. But it worked superbly well. There are all sorts of stories told about that production, how Mac Líammóir fell in love with Marshall, and offered attention to him and that Marshall clocked him in the wings. You've heard that?

NG: No.

JD: People talked incessantly about the things that were going on on the stage and the things that were going on in the wings. All this stuff about Mac Líammóir was very well known. The whole town knew about Mac Líammóir and Edwards, and about Mac Líammóir's relationship with various men, and about the tragic occasion when Mac Líammóir fell in love with the Guard on point duty in O'Connell Street. You've heard?

CM: No.

JD: Yes. He used to stand there like a calf stoned out of its mind, staring at this Guard.

Poster for Blacula (American International Pictures 1972) starring William Marshall.

NG: And the whole traffic stood still?

JD: Not at all. No, everything carried on as normal. Mac Líammóir just stood there outside the Ambassador Cinema and looked across at the Guard waving on the traffic. The Guard's perfect beauty and decorum appealed to Mac Líammóir enormously. And people just felt: God help him, sure, the poor divil.

CM: Can you remember the last time you saw him on stage?

JD: I certainly can. One night not long after Irene and I were married – it must have been '73 or '74 – I saw in the paper, *The Good-Natured Man*, with Micheál Mac Líammóir, last day. I said to Irene, 'Mac Líammóir is looking shook; my guess is that this is the last time he is going to appear on the boards. Let's see if we can get tickets.' So we rang, we got tickets, and we went. Now, in *The Good-Natured Man*, Mac Líammóir played Lofty, the man about town. And as his last speech Lofty says: 'Well, gentlemen, I have a mind to retire. And if any one of the present company is minded to succeed me, let him step forward.'

Marvellous: there's no question but that he

Micheál Mac Líammóir

68

chose the part. I believe Mac Líammóir did play *The Importance of Being Oscar* once after that, but that was the last time he appeared in a play as such. So unfortunately my hunch was right. But that night in *The Good-Natured Man*, I knew he was blind, virtually; I knew he was hardly able to move, and I knew that he couldn't possibly play the part: but I believed him. And one of the few occasions I've really lost my temper was when I was teaching in Glenstall in the 1960s and a whiz kid monk there said to me, 'Oh, Mac Líammóir, he's pure ham, isn't he?' And I thought, well, okay, Mac Líammóir could ham it when he wanted to. He could go on automatic pilot; he had to get through the day just like everybody else. But I became really angry when I was told he was a ham because I had paid good money to see Mac Líammóir in plays where he was not hamming. He was a terrific actor when he put himself out.

Siobhán McKenna in 1985 Druid production of *Bailegangaire*

NG: Ria Mooney, Donal McCann, Cyril Cusack, Micheál Mac Líammóir, these were obviously all major presences for you in theatre. What other great actors were there in your time: Siobhán McKenna?

JD: Yes: once in *Bailegangaire*.

NG: I saw that too.

JD: That's not long before she died; she gave that everything. But she was actually quite a mannered actress, and she shows up terribly badly in film. She can't adjust to the ways of film acting.

NG: The film of *The Playboy* must be really one of the worst ever made!

JD: It's of mythological vileness and badness. 'Oh, it's a terror to be aged a score.' Well, it might be when you're 45.

CM: Were there other outstanding performers for you?

JD: Godfrey Quigley, without doubt: Quigley was an immense actor.

NG: He was. I remember seeing him in *The Gigli Concert*, and I had always admired him before, but that was a performance that seemed to go outside what you thought was possible as his range.

JD: Yes, that's so true. It was astonishing in *The Gigli Concert* the way he broke down, came apart on stage, but the most astonishing thing was the way he then reconstituted himself and presented himself as cured and normal. I mean, that was absolutely staggering because he had been as sick as a dog and then he looked just like a normal person. It's all very well to show somebody going mad and coming apart at the seams; we're all very impressed by that. But that resurrection was the *coup de grâce* as far as I was concerned. His sickness took the form of a longing for transcendence, and it was an infectious sickness. It infected the Man played by Quigley and the Tom Hickey character, J.P.W. King. And at the end of play, King is just as sick, and the audience was as sick as a dog as well. But the Man is back to normal. You remember the scene where he comes in, he's coming in on the left, coming down towards us, and he says: 'how much do I owe you', or words to that effect.

NG: And he's all dolled up because he and the the wife are going for a night out. And he's come in to say thank you to King. And he's so ordinary by that stage. He really does just look like your average gombeen businessman.

JD: You realize in the end of the play that when he wanted to transcend himself, he was reasonably human. But when he's back in character, he's really awful, outside the Pale; you don't want to be like that. That performance in *The Gigli Concert* was exceptional, but Quigley was a very fine actor

Poster for 1983 Abbey production of *The Gigli Concert*

71

all along. In the fifties, he played Macbeth, and a very amusing thing happened the night that I saw it. He did the 'if it were done when 'tis done' soliloquy on the front stage, and at one point he got down on one knee. But he lost himself in it. He kept on 'if it were done when 'tis done, then 'twere well/It was done quickly; if it were done when 'tis done, then 'twere ...' And he kept on going around in circles. The syntax is pretty difficult.

NG: It is desperate.

JD: Now, at that stage we were doing *Macbeth* in school, and I knew every line of the play, and I knew he was in trouble. So, he had a stage dagger and to startle himself, he took out the stage dagger and drove it into his thigh. Then he managed go on to the next line: '... If th' assassination,/Could trammel up the consequences, and catch ...' But when he took out the dagger and made to stab himself, I thought: 'Christ, I hope it's a stage dagger.' He was very good. I had seen McMaster play Macbeth, and McMaster was certainly better, but Quigley was very, very good. Do you know the story about Kubrick and Quigley?

NG: No.

JD: This is actually a good story, and it happens to be true, which is always an advantage on occasions like this. In *Barry Lyndon*, Quigley plays a soldier: he's marching at the head of his men, somebody shoots him, and he falls down and dies. So they started filming at eight o'clock in the morning, and Quigley advanced, he's shot, he puts up his hand, he falls down dead. Kubrick says: 'we'll do it again.' So, Quigley goes, he changes his waistcoat and puts in the sponge with the blood, and he marches again. Same thing happens. Nine o'clock, ten o'clock. They're still doing it at three o'clock in the afternoon. And Quigley goes up to Kubrick, and he says: 'Stanley, I must be doing something wrong. What am I doing wrong?' 'Well', said Kubrick, 'what happens here?' 'I'm shot, and I fall down dead.' 'Yes, but what's the first thing you feel when you're shot?' 'It's bad news, isn't it?' 'There's more than that', says Kubrick. 'Well, what is it?' And Kubrick says to him: 'you feel surprised.' Now if you look at this on screen, that's exactly what happens in the film. Quigley is in the middle of a battle, guns are going off everywhere: he's shot, he knows it's fatal, and he's surprised. He really got the message. In that tiny moment in the film, Quigley communicates the ludicrous sense of being surprised that you're shot in battle. That's true; that's the way it would be.

CM: Were there Quigley performances after *The Gigli Concert*?

JD: There were, but he never equalled that. He played James Tyrone in a revival of *Long Day's Journey into Night* sometime in the 1980s, with Siobhán McKenna. It looked like a cast from heaven, but it was absolutely disastrous. Neither of them could get hold of the dialogue; they couldn't remember the speeches; they were fustering and fidgeting; and they were both near death. And it was sad to see these two great performers really swimming out of their depth and sinking.

CM: There have been a couple of performances we keep circling around in these interviews. If you were curating an anthology of John Devitt's favourite performances and had to pick three, what would they be?

JD: Donal McCann, Godfrey Quigley, and Ria Mooney. Ria Mooney as Mary Tyrone in *Long Day's Journey*: that was the first time in the theatre that I realized that an actor can be like a great pianist. There's something in performance and interpretation that is absolutely mesmeric and deeply moving. I can still feel that performance as if it was yesterday. That was a complete eye-opener to me. Then Donal McCann in *Faith Healer* — that was beyond praise. And Godfrey Quigley in *The Gigli Concert*. Here was an actor I knew was terrific; I'd been watching him since the mid-fifties. He'd been on film and he'd been away; he came back and he did this part. And it was just so bloody generous; he gave everything to that part. I saw that performance a couple of times over a period of about five weeks, and I realized this guy had nowhere to hide. He can't terminate; he can't go off if he isn't up to it. He has to have therefore a tremendous technical resourcefulness just to get through the night. And yet he's got so much more than that. I tried over and over again to describe to people that particular performance; what it was like to be in the theatre watching it. And everybody who saw it had the same feeling about it.

NG: For me the theatrical highlight of the whole thing was that wordless sobbing speech of Quigley's, which isn't a speech, it's just a breakdown on stage. I've never seen anything like that before or since.

JD: Did you think he was going to die?

NG: Well, it looked quite like it.

JD: It really is the case. There was one night I thought he was

Poster for 1980 Abbey production of *Faith Healer*

finished. I didn't think he could get out of it. Nothing I've seen in the theatre or anywhere else compares to that moment and the sense of fear: 'oh my God, he's finished.' Or as we might say in Dublin: 'he's rightly fucked now'.

NG: That sounds like an excellent exit line to me.

Chapter 4
Plays and Playwrights

Tom Murphy

CM: Are there forgotten plays and playwrights from the fifties that we ought to be remembering?

JD: There are a few. Do you know the last new play that was done in the old Abbey in 1951; I didn't see it, but do you know what it was? *The House Under Green Shadows* by Maurice Meldon. And it's an interesting play; he's a guy who's been reading too much Yeats, he's been reading 'Meditations in Time of Civil War' and 'Nineteen Hundred and Nineteen.' Meldon could only have been about 22 or 23 when that play was done. It's a fantastic farrago of Yeatsian stuff, but it's actually quite interesting. And a few years later, he wrote a very interesting play called *Aisling*. It's a kind of carnivalesque play, with a very sour attitude to the inhibiting nature of the new Irish state. You know the play?

CM: Yes.

JD: It is curious. On the one hand, it has a tone that is sparkling and funny, and it makes for a good evening in the theatre; on the other hand, there is something that is sour and sardonic about it. It's not entirely satisfactory, but it is really interesting because it's part of a questioning, asking fundamental questions about theatrical representation, modes of representation.

CM: It's very much questioning realist orthodoxies.

JD: Yes, and prevailing myths, having fun at their expense. But it had this kind of sourness about it that I remember quite vividly. I didn't see the first production of the play in 1953. I saw it when it was revived in the Gate after Meldon's death. He died in a freak accident. Did I mention that?

NG: No.

JD: I only found this out five or six years ago because *Aisling* was revived again, in the Inchicore Technical School, and I'd seen the Gate production in 1958, immediately after Meldon's death. So, nothing would satisfy me but to go out to Inchicore and see it again. And there I met Maurice Meldon's wife, Barbara Kelly, and she came out with this quite fantastic story. Maurice Meldon was a civil servant. He was cycling home from work, when he had a freak accident: he fell off his bike, he hit the curb, and his false teeth were driven back into his throat and he choked. That was the story she told me.

NG: Dear Lord.

JD: I really think Meldon was a bad loss. And rather sadly, he's never mentioned now. But I think he should be mentioned because, even though in the *House Under Green Shadows* he's a man who has succumbed to influences that he cannot control, it and *Aisling* are well worth looking at.

CM: You speak of Meldon not being able to control the influence of Yeats. Were there fifties plays that talked back to the classics of the earlier period?

JD: Well Denis Johnston's play *The Scythe and the Sunset* was intended as a kind of counterweight to *The Plough and the Stars* but it's in fact an inverted tribute.

NG: It's too talky, isn't it?

JD: Yes, it's also too much concerned with exhibiting the Dublin people as curious. That's the thing that has hurt theatre, the idea that the Irish are curious and funny. Well, I'm Irish. I find Irish people and their dilemmas interesting. And I think, particularly in a culture like ours which has been badly damaged by discontinuities of various kinds, a key phase in the evolution of that culture is where people begin to find their experience and that of their neighbours interesting enough and compelling enough to write about and pay attention to. But the idea that Johnston has in that play of exhibiting curious forms of behaviour is really degrading. In other respects I've a lot of time for Johnston, but *The Scythe and the Sunset* ends up making you aware how good *The Plough and the Stars* is by contrast.

NG: The fifties has remained a favourite period for fiction writers. Are there plays from that time that might have influenced them?

JD: I think so. There was a play of Walter Macken's called *Twilight of a Warrior*, for instance. Now, it's not a great play, that's for sure and certain, and Macken couldn't really write the big speeches. He could write the ordinary middle-of-the-road exchanges, but he couldn't write the big speeches.

1958 Abbey Production of *The Scythe and the Sunset* featuring Frainc Mac Mornain and Dennis Brennan.

Nevertheless he had got hold of a subject here, a really interesting subject. And his subject is, in essence, the same subject John McGahern returns to in *Amongst Women*. The affinity between the two is uncannily close.

CM: The revolutionary hero with nowhere to go in post-Independence Ireland?

JD: Just so. There was more political theatre in the period than you might expect. At least there are some plays in the 1950s which deal with the lives of politicians and the kind of crises they face, including one rather bizarre play by Donal Giltinan. Giltinan wrote several plays. I don't know if he's remembered now at all; is he?

CM: Not by very many, no.

JD: Yes, well, quite right and proper: he's no bloody good. But he does deal with politicians who get involved in some sort of crisis. And in one play from the mid-fifties, called, I think, *The Flying Wheel*, he describes a politician who has an accident and covers up. He was anticipating a real-life incident from years later involving a very famous Irish minister who had an accident in Wicklow, also involving a cover-up. At least it was widely believed that when a ministerial Merc crashed in '68 or '69, that the minister was actually driving and his official driver was intoxicated lying on the back seat, and that after the crash, the two switched places. Giltinan's plays were only coincidently about politicians. But there is one play by John McCann, which I think is his best play, called *Early and Often*, which is about cheating in politics. The significance of the title is 'vote early and often' and I remember howling at that because my father as a Guard was well aware of the fact that in certain parts, with PR and multiseat constituencies, the last seat is frequently decided by a handful of votes. So that, if, for example, you vote early and often and you can get the recently deceased to appear and exercise their democratic rights, you can swing that last seat. We were very well aware of that, particularly in the fifties because – here is a bizarre fact about the political nature of the fifties – every government that offered itself for re-election after the war was defeated until 1961. In other words, the general elections of '48, '51, '54, and '57 all brought changes of government. Now, in many cases, these changes could be attributed to the intervention of the dead, or the devoted and repeated votings by enthusiastic party members. McCann's *Early and Often* does touch on that. In fact, he comes very close in the course of that play to a political epiphany, about what you give up to become a politician and about how everybody around you has got to suffer. And then he dodges the logic of it. That represents a lamentable failure of dramatic imagination.

NG: He was extremely popular at the time, McCann, wasn't he?

JD: He was the most frequently performed playwright in the Ernest Blythe regime at the Queen's in the 1950s. The function of his plays was to administer reassurance. The paradox was that the people who went in their thousands to

Portrait of Lord Mayor John McCann by Sean Keating

see his plays knew they were bullshit. For example, everyone who went would have had a relative in England.

CM: Right.

JD: And they would have been in touch with them. But within the frame of reference of those plays, England is a place where people are automatically corrupted and debased and destroyed spiritually and morally. Everybody knew that that wasn't the case. But they sat there pretending. There's something really troubling about that, and about the frequency with which people went to see his plays.

NG: But it was part of a Blythe policy, wasn't it? To have plays that were anodyne, that didn't particularly open up politically sore subjects and so on.

JD: Yes, it might have been, though personally I thought he was more interested in simply getting people into the theatre. And yet there were playwrights who did tackle taboo subjects. Louis D'Alton is a good man to illustrate that point. He was dealing with weird subjects like incest and devastating criticisms of Ireland and its passion. You remember that really good play of his that resembles Shaw; what is it called? *This Other Eden*. That play is very interesting because people have such an exaggerated reverence for the heroes of the recent past that they actually turn them into tailors' dummies. They dehumanize them to a grotesque extent. That play ran for ages in the Abbey and was quite well done.

CM: And made a reasonably good film.

JD: Yes it's not a bad film, it's fairly faithful to the play.

NG: The way history books tell it, the 1960s were the new beginning in Irish theatre. At the time did you have a sense that *Philadelphia, Here I Come!* in 1964 was a landmark play?

JD: No, I didn't feel that, no. I don't think at the time there was a feeling of breakthrough, where will we go next?

CM: But it did represent a change of style, didn't it?

JD: Yes, yes. What was interesting about the play was that you were not being confined to a box. A lot of the materials belonged to naïve realism or naturalism, but what was significant about that production was that you knew that; instead of accepting it as your point of entry into the play, it was something that coloured the way you looked at the play. And that sense of liberation from the box was a liberation from the predictable kinds of naturalism. The end result was that it was tremendously moving – the emotional power of the play was extraordinary. And to be absolutely honest with you, when I re-read that play, I'm baffled. It doesn't read as if it would have that power. There's a much bigger than normal difference between reading that play and seeing it in a good production.

1972 Abbey Production of *Philadelphia, Here I Come!* featuring Ray McAnally and Gerard McSorley.

CM: Would this go back to the sense of an audience and the experience of emigration? You were saying, for instance, that your brother had emigrated to England …

JD: Yes, everybody had an emigrant in the family. When I was at school, I don't think there was a household where there weren't emigrants, mostly in England. And it was a very painful business, particularly when the emigrants returned. I remember my brother coming back in the 1960s and envying me the fact that I'd got a fabulous job teaching English in a monastery school. It was just pure luck, and I was very glad to seize the opportunity. But this was the kind of of job he'd have leapt at. There was the feeling that once they'd gone, they couldn't reinsert themselves. We don't have that feeling any longer.

CM: Were there other plays in that early '60s period that touched a chord for the audiences of the time?

JD: There was Hugh Leonard's adaptation of *A Portrait of the Artist as a Young Man*, *Stephen D*. That was done at the Gate, with Norman Rodway, a terrific actor with a wonderful voice. I'd seen him for years, throughout the late fifties. That was a fairly slick production. There were things done, transitions, adventurous elements in the staging there. And of course, there was the direct address to the audience during the hell-fire sermon. I suppose we were used enough to hell-fire sermons to really relish that one.

NG: You were saying earlier that playwrights such as Louis D'Alton were able to deal with some suprisingly taboo subjects in the 1950s. But the sixties did see some breakthroughs in this area, didn't they, such as Tom Kilroy's *Death and Resurrection of Mr Roche?*

JD: Yes, that was a stunning production: the way that play dealt with things everybody knew about and nobody had previously exhibited in the theatre – the humiliation of people whose sexual orientation was irregular by the standards of the time, the mean-spiritedness of the characters, and the absolutely unblinking quality of the play. I remember the effect of that play rather than the detail of the production, because it was a bit of a shock to the system.

NG: And was the reaction because of the topic or …

JD: No. What I felt was that this is an enlargement, the real thing. With Kilroy's later play, *Talbot's Box*, again there was the sense of a playwright handling radioactive material. That was a very vivid production, because for somebody of my generation, Matt Talbot was a very special figure. I mean, I walked through the streets to school past the house where he lived. I knew exactly where he had died. I knew so much about him. He was the exemplary sinner who redeems himself. But Kilroy's angle on the play was not particularly religious; there was a certain kind of coldness and rigour about the play, and about the production, which startled me. I won't say

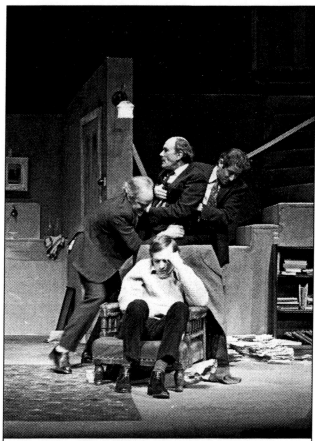

1973 Abbey production of *The Death and Resurrection of Mr Roche* featuring Peadar Lamb, Eamon Kelly, Joe Dowling and Bosco Hogan

85

alienated me, but startled me. I expected a play about the Matt Talbot I had been taught to admire and revere. And instead of that I saw something altogether colder; and at the same time, I couldn't deny that John Molloy, who gave a great performance in the central role, was right inside that part. I can still feel how strange and uncanny he was in the resurrection scene.

NG: When you move into the 1970s, there are some hard-hitting plays of Friel, also, aren't there, like *The Mundy Scheme*, did you see that?

JD: No, I missed it, I missed it. It was on in the Olympia and it was booked out the one night I could go: I couldn't get in. And it's never been done again.

NG: What about *The Gentle Island*, also from the early 1970s?

JD: Yes. I didn't see the original production of that, but I saw it in the Peacock revival. That's a terrifying play: that's one of his seriously upsetting plays. What is so disturbing about it is the notion of the violence inside you. *The Gentle*

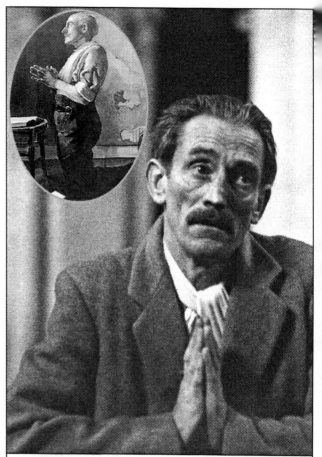

1977 Peacock production of *Talbot's Box* featuring John Molloy as Matt Talbot. Inset: Devotional image of Talbot.

Island, was there ever a title that proved more deceptive? I'll tell you another play of Friel that struck me as having a real bearing: *Living Quarters*. I went to it by accident. I was going home from the library one night; I had no intention of going to it, I just thought if there's a seat, I'll go. And I went in and sat there on my own, and I was absolutely exhilarated by it. Micheal O' hAonghusa gave a great performance in it as the priest who is not equal to the spiritual role that he's been assigned. It was this man who is actually past it but who's pretending he's not past it. He's light on his feet, he's dancing around, he's very active, and then wham! He's hit with the fact that he's past it. The play is quite cruel really in saying all that - it's an icicle of a play.

CM: It's a good description. It was a rich period for Friel, wasn't it, with *The Freedom of the City* before *Living Quarters*, and *Aristocrats* coming immediately afterwards?

JD: Yes, that was in '78 or '79. That was another great performance, by the way – John

ABBEY THEATRE OPENS 8 MARCH 1979

INGRID CRAIGIE · KATE FLYNN · BILL FOLEY · GEOFF GOLDEN · JOHN KAVANAGH · KEVIN McHUGH
DEARBHLA MOLLOY · NIALL O'BRIEN · STEPHEN REA · DIRECTOR JOE DOWLING · DESIGN WENDY SHEA

BRIAN FRIEL'S NEW PLAY
ARISTOCRATS

Kavanagh as Casimir in that play was preternaturally good. I remember I went on the Wood Quay march and I ended up marching along with Kavanagh and he was talking about Friel. He said acting in Friel was just glorious because the thing was so phrased that the actor was being instructed without being tyrannized over or dominated. There was one way the speech would go, and you could find it out if you stayed with it long enough.

CM: To go back to *The Freedom of the City* for a moment: did you see the first production in 1973?

JD: Yes, I saw both the original and a later production.

CM: Do you remember the impact; was there a sense that this is theatre that is doing something that needs to be done?

JD: Yes, it was responding to a specific occasion. Bloody Sunday was devastating, it was really difficult. Anyone who was living anywhere in Ireland was devastated: it was the one thing that stopped people. And then the amazing folly of the British government and the British media in dealing with it, their utter stupidity: they began to treat us like half-wits, as if we had no power and no intelligence. It was a bad, bad, bad business. But the play addressed that, and did it in a very interesting kind of way. I don't think it's the play of Friel's that will live longest. By the time it was revived in the 1990s, the life seemed to be leaking away from it because it was so bound up with the occasion. But it certainly had local life.

NG: What about Field Day in the 1980s: did their plays make much of an impact on you?

JD: Well, there was no way of missing one of their productions: nobody in their right mind would miss them. I remember the excitement of the first production of *Translations* was colossal. It was partly the cast: Ray McAnally again as the teacher – I mean, what a performance. It was effortless. You can only do that sort of thing if you've served an apprenticeship of 40 years to acting. *Translations* had the force of a political pamphlet, and it acted like a kind of synopsis, a metonymy for the whole 19th century. The play is supposed to be set in the mid-1830s but there are bits and pieces of much later in the 19th century leaking into it. And of course, Friel was able to do in it the usual Friel trick of finding one theatrical convention and exploiting it brilliantly, in this case English being simultaneously English and Irish. It was just terrific. Yet, at the same time, when I saw *Faith Healer* a few months later, I thought: 'no, *Translations* is top of the second division in Friel, and *Faith Healer* is top of the first division.' That's the way I felt about the comparative value of the two plays.

CM: What were the other highlights of Field Day for you?

JD: Kilroy's *Double Cross* I thought was really interesting. That was taking a look at aspects of Irish life and Irish history that nobody'd paid much attention to, with the exception of Charles Lysaght, an old mate of mine, who wrote a biography of Brendan Bracken. It's a fascinating book, and a fascinating subject, combined in the play with the figure of William Joyce, the broadcaster 'Lord Haw-Haw'. It raises questions like the book on treason by Rebecca West: what is your connection to any society? What kind of loyalties does it demand? These are the issues that aren't directly vocalized in the play, but hit you on the way home. I mean *Double Cross* is like a bomb with a delayed action. It opens up a whole set of questions, which I think is what Field Day was primarily about. But in theatre terms, also, *Double Cross* was really arresting. I don't know if they did it in every production, but when the play was done in the Gate, at the end of the first act, Stephen Rea has his back to the audience, and he's been impersonating Bracken. And he turns around, after about five seconds, and he's Joyce. There was something really weird; that was really a shock, with funny feelings at the back of your neck. I thought, my God, I didn't realize that one was plural. I always thought one was singular. It was incredible, and it was done by sheer force of will and talent. It was one of the great theatre moments.

NG: Perhaps one of the most interesting Field Day plays was the one that got away. Frank McGuiness's *Observe the Sons of Ulster Marching Towards the Somme* was apparently originally offered to Field Day, and they turned it down.

JD: What a difference it would have made if they had done it. It would have been absolutely fascinating to see them do that play. Why did that play work so very well? I remember going to it with my late brother, and he was extraordinarily arrested by it. He was upset about the frequency of homosexual reference in the play. But he was riveted by the fact that an Irish playwright was

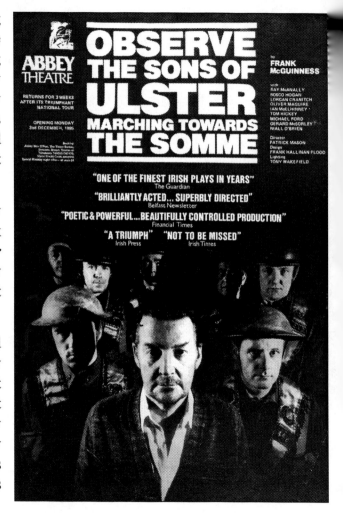

addressing this problem because our grandfather had fought in Gallipoli and in the Boer War, in fact; and retired from the army finally when he was stationed in what is now Iraq. So there was a whole dimension to the history of the family that in some way was shadowed, or faintly reflected, or made accessible through that play. But the last act of the play is wonderful. Just take that final scene where the rivers of Ulster are being invoked. You're in this small theatre – it was originally staged in the Peacock, though it transferred up to the Abbey – you're looking at a tiny, cramped space. And what is happening is that your imagination is literally being flooded with suggestion.

NG: Yes. The technical daring, it seems to me, of *Observe the Sons of Ulster* is the fact you never hear a gun, never once.

JD: Yes. The funny thing is, I never noticed that until you said it. And the reason I never noticed it is I'm pretty sure I heard guns: they went off in my head. At least, I saw those guys being shot down; that's for certain sure. And I was in grief. That's theatre: where the available means are far out of proportion to the effect produced. There's no way of explaining it, it's a real mystery.

NG: It's obvious that Tom Murphy's work has had a very special impact on you.

JD: You can't know Ireland unless you know Murphy, in my view. At one stage I read a lot of sociologists writing about literature, as if literature were a branch of sociology. They talk about representations, very often representations of women: there's something really suspect about that. What is really interesting is when you're being invited to respond in the theatre to a work where the nature of reality is not clearly fixed and absolutely known; it cannot be boxed. If you look at the drama of the fifties, you can see that there was a kind of excessive confidence in what constitutes reality; therefore we didn't need to inspect our conventions of understanding or presentation. Now, that's the change that Murphy represents to me. Murphy plays fast and loose with those well-understood conventions that were in most plays of the fifties. And he's therefore able to go places and take you places that the more realist dramatist cannot go.

CM: Let's look at some examples. What was the Murphy play that first really featured for you?

JD: *Famine*. His first big success, *A Whistle in the Dark*, was not staged at the Abbey – Ernest Blythe saw to that – so I didn't get to see it until later. So it was *Famine*.

NG: Did you see the original production in the Peacock in 1968?

JD: Yes. *Famine* was the unspeakable thing. There has been a lot of bullshit talked about the Famine since 1996 or 1997 or whenever the commemoration took place. The fact of the matter is that my father was from rural Ireland and my mother was from Dublin, and they had been touched by the Famine. When I would come in and eat a big meal, my mother would say: you must have walked on hungry grass. Hungry grass was the grass that grew out of the graves of the dead. There were things like that and the fear of the poorhouse that James Tyrone talks about in *Long Day's Journey into Night*. The poorhouse was still frequently mentioned in the fifties, but it had vanished from the conversation by the late sixties. 'Oh, we'll end up in the poorhouse.' 'Do you think I'm made of money? We'll end up in the poor house.' Murphy's play, with its weird effects and Brechtian short scenes, brought the shocking discovery that our ancestors were victims but they were also victimizing. The way in which the victims victimized is not part of the conventional wisdom about the Famine. It's not what I learned about the Famine in the scattered references to it in history books in school. What is disconcerting and exciting about Murphy is that he pushes you beyond what you thought you knew.

NG: It's partly a matter of style, isn't it?

JD: Absolutely. Take *The Morning after Optimism*, for instance. I remember going for a drink, one afternoon in a pub, right across from the Abbey where they were staging the play in 1971. And who wandered in but Colin Blakely who played the lead in that production. He was in there having a pint, and I got talking to him. And I said to him: 'God, that's some performance you're giving over there: all these little darts of energy around the stage.' The fact was, you felt that he didn't know the next sentence, that it was all being invented on the hoof. They often say about a work of art that it's inchoate, meaning that it's unfinished. Well, the quick glory of the theatre is that moment by moment, it's inchoate. It's only when you get to the end that you're able to realize it's a finished thing, that it is properly shaped. It's caught in that phrase from *Hamlet* where the First or Second Gentleman describes Ophelia's speech in her madness. It's in the fourth act.

Abbey Theatre
From 7 June 1977

Ray McAnally   Rosaleen Linehan
Stephen Brennan   Bernadette Shortt
in
Thomas Murphy's

The Morning after Optimism

Director Jonathan Hales
Design Bronwen Casson

Poster for 1977 Abbey revival of
The Morning After Optimism

NG: 'Her speech is nothing,/Yet the unshaped use of it doth move / The hearers to collection.'

JD: It's a fascinating sentence that always struck me as applying with terrific force to Murphy's plays. On one occasion I was chairperson of the Association of Teachers of English, and we invited Murphy along to give a reading from *The Morning after Optimism*. He produced a text alright, and he put it on the podium but he didn't use the text. He knew the thing by heart, and he was a wonderful reader of his own work. There's some kind of verse there, with its own rhythm. It isn't something imposed from outside but it has its own rhythm. And as a result a bum note from an actor in a Murphy play is disastrous.

NG: He takes a lot of risks, Murphy, doesn't he, and not all the risks pay off.

JD: Right. But even some of his failures are interesting like *The Blue Macushla*. I know that's not a good play. But I can't feel it because I had a hell of a time watching it. I loved the look and feel of it. It looked like a Hollywood film noir, with serious metaphysical pretensions. The point about the play is that it is the *ne plus ultra* of gangsterism infesting politics. *The Blue Macushla* would bear looking at for anyone with sensitive political antennae.

NG: Murphy doesn't make things easy for his producers, does he? There's *A Thief of a Christmas*, another spectacular flop when first produced, but a potentially extraordinary play, if you can manage to muster a cast of some 45, who have to laugh onstage for most of the performance.

JD: That play has one of those great theatrical moments, the scene where all the hands go up in the air, and they're calling down more grief, more pain, more sorrow. It's hilarious, like something out of the Middle Ages. That's something you could never get out of your system if you saw it. It's a shame to do *Bailegangaire* without doing its companion piece *A Thief of a Christmas* in some proximity to it.

NG: *A Thief of a Christmas* was in fact staged at the Abbey within a month of the Druid Theatre production of *Bailegangaire* coming to the Gaiety. They were on at nearly the same time.

JD: They're such completely different plays; they're so utterly at odds with each other in their modes of presentation. But the way they play in your mind, the way they talk to each other in your mind, is fascinating. In *Bailegangaire*, the construction of the narrative is the essence of the drama, whereas the enactment is the essence of *A Thief of a Christmas*.

NG: I hope that I will live to see the day when they have *A Thief of a Christmas* on the main stage of the Abbey and *Bailegangaire* in the Peacock.

CM: To get back to where we started with the sociological importance of Murphy's work, what about

1985 World Premiere of *A Thief of a Christmas* at The Abbey

The House in 2000? I know you've written on it and you've spoken on it before. What was it about *The House* that you thought made it such an important production?

JD: Well, I don't think it's his best play. But I do think it's a play where Murphy tries to say a lot of things about Ireland as it evolved from roughly the mid-fifties to the year 2000. It's a very sardonic play; it's a very cold play, in many respects. But then it has a few little moments of tenderness between people we have learned to despise, little farewells and little nuances. And in the feeling about seeking out property and possession, it catches something important that happened in Ireland, something that happens to Christy, the central figure in the play. Christy himself is aware of it. It's like Angelo in *Measure for Measure* who never lies to himself. Christy is like that; he has that kind of ruthless capacity. It's as though he says, damn it, it's the truth, so let's have it. I think it's a play that Murphy deliberately crafted so that it would be like that; it would constitute some sort of statement about Ireland and how it's changed. That's something that strikes me generally about Murphy. In ordinary polite conversation there are constraints; there are things that don't get said. The things that don't and cannot and shouldn't get said in polite conversation, in Murphy these things get said. And *The House* is full of them. People making their career as pimps in London; people selling out on property; the nostalgic prostitute who is appalled that the house is going to be sold – it was the one fixed point in her universe. If we were in Tuam or Ennis, we wouldn't open a conversation in a pub by talking about such things, but they get forthrightly spoken in Murphy. And that quality is particularly strong in *The House*. When I reviewed the play, I called my review 'In Around the House.' Do you know the origin of that expression?

CM: No.

JD: The house in a Gaelic football field is the goal, goal-post and crossbar. So, 'in around the house' means 'get in around the house; lurry into them; knock hell out of them.' And it struck me that the competition for the house in the play has all the ferocity of a Gaelic football match gone wrong. *The House* in Murphy's output is the bookend for *A Whistle in the Dark*. *A Whistle in the Dark* is a sort of vertical cross-section taken at a particular moment, and *The House* is a more reflective, more concentrated, deliberately more synoptic account of a much longer period. It has that quality of a summing up of everything that Murphy has to say about Ireland since the fifties.

TOM MURPHY

The House

Cover of Tom Murphy's *The House*

Chapter 5
Theatre and Religion

Sarah-Jane Drummey in 2001 Abbey Theatre
production of *The Sanctuary Lamp*

NG: You spoke in one of our earlier conversations about a 'vestigial religious reverence' of the audience in relation to the theatre. Was there a time when it was less 'vestigial', when there would have been greater awareness of the religious dimension to drama?

JD: I think so. Take Brendan Behan's *The Quare Fellow*: I now think of it as the most completely misunderstood play. My father and mother saw it in the theatre, and insisted that I listen to it on the radio. When I had listened to it, they said: 'well, what do you think of that?' And I said: 'I think that's tremendous. God, that's powerful.' Now, we didn't talk about capital punishment or hanging offences, or any of that stuff. What we talked about was the doctrine of the Mystical Body. The Mystical Body doctrine is that we don't see or know Christ, or God, except through other living human beings who compose his body. That was what struck my father and mother and struck me immediately. We were hearing sermons about the Mystical Body and its integrity, and why every member of the Mystical Body was entitled to respect because it all composes Christ. And that of course, is *The Quare Fellow*, isn't it?

Advertisement for 1956 Theatre Royal Production of Behan's *The Quare Fellow.*

CM: Yes, I suppose so.

JD: When you think about it, the Quare Fellow is never seen, but he is completely knowable in and through the members who are scattered around in the prison. My father, my mother, and myself, the three of us were absolutely unanimous. We didn't discuss this; this was a point of departure. Wasn't that an interesting way of treating the doctrine of the Mystical Body? It just seemed self-evident.

CM: Presumably for someone of your generation and background that sort of awareness of Catholic doctrine would have been taken for granted?

JD: Just so. You remember in *Long Day's Journey* where Tyrone claims Shakespeare was an Irish Catholic? I know that's regarded as a tremendously laughable thing, but that's the way I grew up. I was instructed at school in Shakespeare as an Irish Catholic.

NG: Fairly seriously?

JD: Oh yes. There were all the references to the Catholic sacraments in *Hamlet* and *Macbeth*, in particular. One example is when Macduff announces the death of Duncan:

> Most sacrilegious murder had broke ope
> The Lord's anointed temple and stole thence
> The life o'th' building.

The life of the building is the consecrated Host. In school, it was simply taken for granted that Shakespeare was a Catholic, and not necessarily an Irishman but quite probably an Irishman. Look at how good he was for a start. But certainly all the references to the sacraments, which were startlingly frequent in the plays, and the feeling of the sacrilegious impending. It seemed obvious to me. That's why I was hugely amused recently, in the last five or ten years, by all this new biographical enthusiasm for Shakespeare's Catholicism. 'Sure,' I said. 'Look, we knew that in O'Connell's School in the fifties.'

NG: There needs no scholar come from Stratford to tell us that.

JD: Exactly so. When I went to college and read *King Lear*, we had some lectures on *King Lear* that were actually immensely useful but avoided all the great issues in the play. Hogan was the professor of English, and he glossed the play, line by line, over a period of about two months. But the thing that immediately struck me was the presentation of Cordelia in that play. A Catholic signs himself thus: on the forehead, on the lips, and in the heart in preparing to hear the gospel. That's what Cordelia represents: a perfect harmony of thought, utterance, and feeling. In the fourth act, there are a couple of references where she is associated with a female version of Christ – when the First Gentleman describes how 'she shook / The holy water from her heavenly eyes' or when she echoes Christ's own words, 'O dear father,/It is thy business that I go about'. That struck me as gilding the lily, pointing up what was already obvious. I know that the play is set in pre-Christian England, but it is also clear that Cordelia is a coded reference to this practice of signing. I remember, when Bishop Neary was still in Maynooth, and he was a liturgical specialist, I asked him: 'is it conceivable that if Shakespeare attended mass at any time in Stratford, say in the 1570s, he would have signed himself thus.' So he launched himself on a couple of months of liturgical investigation, and he sent me a letter telling me it was very likely. So the notion that Shakespeare is penetrated by a particularly Catholic notion of the sacramental, and a particularly Catholic form of reverence, seems to me self-evident. Of course, there are other things in Shakespeare, but it's an element in Shakespeare, of which I was conscious from day one of studying the tragedies.

NG: Was there a time when you felt this sort of religious awareness disappeared from Irish theatre audiences?

JD: In the 1950s, early 1960s, I think there was still a kind of shared system of values – that's perhaps not quite right, rather a shared sense of what was important. That broke down in the 1960s and early 1970s, and with it the religious ethos of the country changed. It is interesting: people think that happened quite recently because of scandals and so forth. But in the mid-sixties, there was a report on the future of the religious in Irish education: it was known by its acronym as the FIRE Report. And already the outlook was very grim; indeed, the place I work in, Mater Dei, was founded specifically because the outlook was so grim and it was going to be necessary to train lay people. There was a definite shift at this time. My sort of understanding of *The Quare Fellow*, for example, simply didn't happen in the productions of it I saw in the new Abbey. There was absolutely no sense that the subtext of this play was the religious mystery of the body of Christ; that didn't exist. It was simply a study in penology. I'm putting this rather clumsily because I haven't really thought it through, but I think there were social, economic, religious changes, and you couldn't really assume that people shared your values as readily as you could a matter of ten years earlier. These convulsions in the sixties weren't visible in the public life of the country, the commemorations, the Dáil and the political debates. But they were in the body of citizens; they were there in the behaviour of people.

NG: Were these changes in belief reflected in the plays produced by the generation of dramatists who lived through them?

JD: Yes, the most striking case would be *Talbot's Box* which we talked about earlier. To understand a response to that play, you have to understand what it was like to be brought up as a Dublin Catholic in the 1940s and 1950s, to be constantly presented with the story of Matt Talbot as an exemplary story, and to pray that he would achieve full canonisation, and to know the precise spot where he died, marked, until quite recently, with flowers. Every time I passed it until about five years ago, it was adorned with flowers. And the house he lived in is demolished. The unmistakable thing is that Talbot existed, was a human being, and his life was a kind of experiment. But all his habits; his habit of going into Holy Cross College in Clonliffe, his habit of self-denial – I realized very early on that he was so extreme. This, I think, is what interested Kilroy: his whole life is an exercise in extremism of a kind only provoked by somebody who's so animated by faith, or by that lively duet, faith and doubt. And what comes out in the play is that the livelier twin is doubt. The play seemed to treat Matt Talbot's life as an astonishing experiment, the result of which is uncertain, whereas ten years earlier, it would have been difficult to have conceived of Matt Talbot's life other than as an extraordinary vindication of a spiritual commitment, at enormous cost and with great pain.

NG: Were there other playwrights with this non-religious interest in religion at the time?

JD: Again we are back to Murphy. At the end of *Bailegangaire*, Mommo starts quoting from the 'Salve Regina'. And it's obvious that Murphy has carried this stuff around in his head. It seems to me that Murphy is one of those guys like McGahern, whether he believes in

God or the Pope doesn't matter a damn. But he knows that the story that is told there is a big story, and it's big enough to set against the tragic and awful aspects of human existence. Whereas most human utterance is simply humiliated by the horror, the 'Salve Regina' is not humiliated by the horror. It's an extraordinary poetic prayer, and Murphy knows that. A lot of his drama has that kind of religious impulse; he's a man of large imagination.

CM: In a sense, that's what O'Neill provided in the 1950s.

JD: Yes, absolutely. Particularly in *Long Day's Journey into Night*, when Mary Tyrone enters in the last act, what's she looking for? She's looking for faith. She's too far gone to do anything but look; even if it was there, she wouldn't be able to recognize it. But she is looking for faith, and faith is not negligible, and the story that the faithful tell is not negligible.

NG: Mary does specifically talk about that, doesn't she, some day Our Lady will forgive me and then I will be able to re-find my faith?

JD: That's true. And she wasn't the only one. Mary Tyrone with her childhood dream of going into the convent introduced me to the sad facts of life, which is that every Catholic girl I approached in the 1950s, in any capacity, wanted to be a nun, and you had to negotiate that before you could make any progress at all. So almost your first line had to be: where did you want to be a nun? What order did you want to join?

> **Salve Regina**
> Hail, holy Queen, Mother of Mercy,
> our life, our sweetness and our hope.
> To thee do we cry, poor banished children of Eve;
> to thee do we send up our sighs,
> mourning and weeping in this vale of tears.
> Turn then, most gracious advocate,
> thine eyes of mercy toward us;
> and after this our exile,
> show unto us the blessed fruit of thy womb, Jesus.
> O clement, O loving, O sweet Virgin Mary.

NG: It's a very different opening gambit from the usual invitation to come up and see your etchings. I wonder, though, how far these non-religious plays about religion, *Talbot's Box*, or Murphy's *The Sanctuary Lamp*, also from the 1970s, were felt to be anti-clerical. It seems to me that both *Talbot's Box* and *Sanctuary Lamp* are plays about spiritual experience that have, as part of their imaginative recreation of that spiritual experience, a kind of kickback at the church as an institution. There are the very virulent speeches of Francisco in *Sanctuary Lamp*, for instance, and the treatment of the figure of the priest in *Talbot's Box*. I am interested in whether that was still felt to be scandalous and shocking, or whether there was an acceptance.

JD: It would have been more shocking in the Murphy play, perhaps because a different audience went to the Abbey, where *The Sanctuary Lamp* was staged, than went to the Peacock, where they put on *Talbot's Box*. Only real crazy people, real infatuates, went to the Peacock. The very suggestion that these things could be dealt with in the theatre in this kind of doom-laden prophetic voice struck some people as outrageous. There was a debate in the Abbey occasioned by *The Sanctuary Lamp*. Famously Cearbhall O'Dálaigh went along and described the play as a masterpiece. There were expressions of outrage at that – 'who does he think he is?' – that kind of thing. But at the same time, these were expressions of outrage by people who had responded to the play, and they had a perfect right to respond to the play in that way. I wouldn't have agreed with that response, but I certainly would have had a good handshake and a cup of tea or maybe even a small whiskey with the guy who said it. I often feel that way about theatrical dispute; that it's a terrific thing, provided it doesn't lead to atrocious acts of violence. It shows people caring about the theatre and caring about the community in which the theatre is happening.

CM: And *Talbot's Box*, was it perceived as anticlerical?

JD: Anticlericalism is a funny thing. To be anticlerical is not to be anti-Catholic; people lived fairly comfortably with negative portrayals of the clergy, or even vicious satires on the clergy. That's okay: they can take it. The thing about these two plays – and this is more striking in relation to *Talbot's Box* – is that Irish Catholicism had generally been understood as a set of answers, reassuring answers which were the foregone conclusions of all your thoughts and all your experiences. That is exactly what doesn't happen in *Talbot's Box*. It's kind of unsettling. I was thinking recently about what was the most influential book in 20th-century Ireland. I'll tell you what it was: Sheehan's *Apologetics*. The book is actually marvellously well written and brilliantly organized, but it was written by a man who was superbly confident that he had the answers. And every Catholic school kid who made it into the senior cycle in my generation – in other words, the supposed leaders of society, those who went into the civil service and those who had most influence on public opinion – would have been saturated in Sheehan's *Apologetics*. For two years we would have spent an hour a week poring over Sheehan's *Apologetics*, in a debating sort of fashion. And as I say, it was the confidence with which the answers were articulated that was most striking about it. That would have been the common experience, right down to the mid-sixties. Then it changed. That was the thing about *Talbot's Box* that was so interesting. It put questions. Maybe Talbot's experiment in living led to something, and maybe it didn't; maybe it was only an experiment that didn't actually have a spiritual bonus attaching. That was something like the force of the play, and the people who went to the Peacock would have taken it in that way. Whereas the people who went to the Abbey and saw *The Sanctuary Lamp*, a significant number of those were offended by it. They were seriously upset by it because terrible things were being said.

CM: You were saying previously that the sense of shared religious values was disappearing much earlier than most people realised?

JD: Already in the early eighties, Peter Connolly, Head of the English Department in Maynooth, knew what was coming. He was our external examiner in Mater Dei and he used to come out and do a bit of work in our living room. He said to me, 'Catholicism will vanish in Ireland in the next generation'. I thought at the time: he's crazy. The poor guy's finally flipped his lid; he's gone; we'd better get him out; I hope he makes it home. But he was proved right. In the last ten or fifteen years, the disappearance of the religious imperative, or even the religious penumbra, so to speak, from the public life of the country is startling by its very completeness.

NG: So those plays of the late seventies by Murphy and Kilroy and Friel you might say were pre-post-Catholic?

JD: That's right. They're much more interesting for that very reason; they have a complicated allegiance to a complex truth. I wonder, could you say something of the same about the Shakespearean period, say 1595 to 1610? Something is leaking away from the audience, but it's still there, and it can still be touched. This would account for the way the sacraments are used in *Hamlet*, for example, or the really bizarre notion in *Macbeth* that the dead Duncan is a consecrated host in a Catholic church. It's the last place in the world you'd expect to find that image, at that time, and yet the audience is still obviously in some way capable of responding to it. But nevertheless, a huge religious and cultural change, an irresistible one, is taking place, and nearly finished. Is the theatre the art form of the eleventh hour, when some things are fading and other things are replacing them, but the things that are fading are still vestigial presences?

CM: They are still there to be used?

JD: Yes. But you can't get them by the old means. You've got to reinvent conventions, and restore them or bend them, in order to get hold of it. That would maybe explain why it's quite a specific period. From the time I got married in 1973 until *Bailegangaire* in the mid-eighties, the theatre was just so charged with life. It was such an extraordinary privilege to be living in the city at that time and able to go and see all of these wonderful plays.

CM: This sense that you're talking about, using the language of liturgy torn free from its contexts, it would make sense with a play like *Sanctuary Lamp*, it would make sense with *Talbot's Box*, and it would make sense even with *Faith Healer*, which we keep coming back to, all of which are written within a few years of each other.

JD: That's why I think the creation of an audience is one of the great things a theatre does. There was a ten year period, the mid-seventies to the mid-eighties, where things were more or less right, and the audience was more or less equal to work and responsive enough to suggestion. I don't have that feeling now. Still, I go to the theatre in hope. And I have had moments of revelation and moments of such pleasure. The pleasure of the theatre is just so enormous. I go to the theatre and I'm looking at a play, and it's called *Faith Healer* or it's called *The Gigli Concert*, and I'm sitting there, and after two or three minutes, all my backache and indecision disappears and I have complete confidence in this, and I know I'm not going to be betrayed. Some dim sense of the whole is implicit in your response to every bit of it, every one of the parts. How does that happen? I don't know. We're talking here about something very mysterious.

108